BLOCK 1B   LITHOSPHERE GEOPHYSICS IN BRITAIN

Prepared by Geoff Brown for the Course Team

CONTENTS

The S339 Course Team

Chairman
Richard Thorpe

Course Manager
Val Russell

Authors
Steve Blake
Geoff Brown
Rob Butler
Steve Drury
Nigel Harris
Chris Hawkesworth
Richard Thorpe

Editors
Gerry Bearman
David Tillotson

Designer
Sarah Powell

Graphic Artists
Sue Dobson
Ray Munns

BBC
Andrew Crilly
David Jackson
Nick Watson

The Open University
Walton Hall, Milton Keynes
MK7 6AA

First published 1990

Designed by the Graphic Design Group of the Open University.

Typeset and printed in Great Britain by Henry Ling Ltd, The Dorset Press, Dorchester, Dorset.

ISBN 0 7492 5019 4

This Block forms part of an Open University course: S339 Understanding the Continents. The complete list of Blocks is on the back cover. If you have not enrolled on the course and would like to buy this or other Open University material, please write to Open University Educational Enterprises Ltd, 12 Cofferidge Close, Stony Stratford, MK11 1BY, Great Britain. If you wish to enquire about enrolling as an Open University student, please write to The Admissions Office, The Open University, PO Box 48, Walton Hall, Milton Keynes, MK7 6AB, Great Britain.

Table A   Scientific terms and concepts introduced or developed in Block 1B

4

OBJECTIVES FOR BLOCK 1B

When you have completed Block 1B, you should be able to:

1 Define and use, or recognize correct definitions of, each of the terms listed in Table A.

2 Distinguish between active and passive techniques in the application of geophysical methods.

3 Explain the principles involved in (a) the application and (b) the interpretation of geophysical surveys, using (i) regional gravity and (ii) regional magnetic data.

4 Given maps showing variations of the (a) Bouguer gravity and (b) aeromagnetic fields, distinguish the regional and residual fields, and comment on the physical characteristics, depth, size and shape of rock units responsible for anomalies.

5 Using the UK Bouguer and magnetic anomaly maps, write an account of regional trends, anomaly patterns and gradient variations within a specified area in relation to the regional geology.

6 Show how gravity and magnetic techniques may be used to evaluate the physical characteristics and subsurface form of a given igneous intrusion/intrusive complex.

7 Use gravity and magnetic data to comment on the shape and thickness of a sedimentary basin.

8 Explain how seismic refraction experiments may be used to determine layered models for crustal/mantle structure within and around the UK.

9 Describe how seismic refraction data have been used to derive a model for crustal structure below the Scottish Midland Valley.

10 Give an account of how seismic reflection profiles are determined and how they may be used for seismic modelling of continental crustal sections.

11 Explain how seismic reflection profiling has contributed to knowledge of (a) crustal and upper mantle structure of the northern UK, and (b) the identification and definition of the Iapetus Suture along the Shannon–Solway line, and (c) the structure of the Variscan terrane of southwest England.

12 Show how seismic data may be used to evaluate the brittle–plastic–ductile model for lithosphere rheology (*cf.* Block 1A, Section 2.2).

1   INTRODUCTION AND STUDY COMMENT

In this, the second part of Block 1, our attention turns to geophysical techniques appropriate for studying the structure and evolution of the lithosphere, which we shall apply to the specific case of Britain. These techniques are particularly useful, because they extend our knowledge of surface geology into the third dimension; they exploit variations in physical properties between different rock types. You will have met almost all these techniques before in your foundation and second level studies, but to appreciate the significance and limitations of geophysical data and interpretations, we shall remind you briefly about their principles and applications. Remember, however, as you read on, that it is the *results* that concern us most, for many of the really exciting recent discoveries about lithospheric processes have depended as much on geophysics as they have on other branches of the Earth sciences. In addition to the printed text, there are several other components to this Block. The coloured potential field maps (Aeromagnetic and Bouguer gravity anomaly) will be used as a data base at various points in Section 2. You will also need to refer to the Geological Survey's Ten Mile Maps, the Colour Plate Booklet (Plates 1.1 and 1.2), and in Section 3 you will be studying the reduced scale NEC seismic section. You will need to view the videocassette sequence *Fragments of Britain* (VC 271) at various points mentioned in the text.

2   POTENTIAL FIELD STUDIES

2.1   AN INTRODUCTION TO GEOPHYSICAL METHODS

Geophysical methods can be divided broadly into two categories, **passive techniques** and **active techniques**. The former exploit natural variations in physical properties that can be measured with instruments at the Earth's surface (e.g. gravity, magnetism), whereas active techniques generally require an artificial energy source (e.g. explosion seismology, resistivity). Each of the techniques is aimed at locating *contrasts* between the physical properties of subsurface rocks. The parameters measured at the surface and the physical property(s) on which the methods depend are shown in Table 2.1. For those three techniques that we shall use in our study of the British lithosphere, Table 2.2 gives typical values for the relevant physical properties of some common rock types. These properties are given as ranges rather than average values, because they vary with rock composition, porosity, degree of saturation, degree of fracturing, groundwater salinity, etc. Unfortunately, the range of values for one rock type is sometimes greater than the difference in values between rock types, and hence a certain value cannot necessarily be considered uniquely useful for diagnosis.

Table 2.1 Geophysical methods with corresponding parameters measured and physical properties

Method	Measured parameter	Physical property, contrasts of which are being detected
Gravity	Spatial variations in the acceleration due to gravity	Density
Magnetic	Spatial variations in the strength of the magnetic field	Magnetic susceptibility and remanence (reflecting, respectively, magnetism induced or frozen into rocks)
Seismic	Travel times of reflected/refracted seismic waves	Velocity of seismic waves (determined by density and elastic moduli)
Resistivity	The variation of electrical potential in the ground when a large current is introduced across the area of interest	Electrical conductivity or resistivity —the two are inversely related

Table 2.2   Physical properties of some common rock types

Rock type	Density/10^3 kg m^{-3}		$10^{-6} \times$ magnetic susceptibility*		Compressional wave speed/km s^{-1}
	Range	Average	Range	Average	Range
Sedimentary					
sandstone	1.61–2.76	2.35	0–1 600	30	2.0–6.0
shales	1.77–3.20	2.40	5–1 480	50	1.5–4.2
limestone	1.93–2.90	2.55	2–280	25	2.0–6.0
Igneous					
rhyolite	2.35–2.70	2.52	20–3 000	50	~3.3
andesite	2.40–2.80	2.61	50–10 000	7 000	variable
granite	2.50–2.81	2.64	0–4 000	200	5.5–6.0
diorite	2.72–2.99	2.85	50–10 000	7 000	6.0–6.6
basalt	2.70–3.30	2.99	20–14 500	6 000	variable
gabbro	2.70–3.50	3.03	80–7 200	6 000	6.5–7.0
peridotite	2.78–3.37	3.15	7 600–15 600	13 000	7.5–8.5
Metamorphic					
quartzite	2.50–2.70	2.60	0–2 000	350	5.5–6.0
schist	2.39–2.90	2.64	25–240	120	variable
granulite	2.52–2.73	2.65	highly variable		5.5–7.0
marble	2.60–2.90	2.75	10–1 000	100	5.0–6.0
slate	2.70–2.90	2.79	0–3 000	500	3.5–4.5
gneiss	2.59–3.00	2.80	10–2 000	1 000	5.5–6.5

*Because we are using SI units, these are just numbers.

ITQ 2.1   To illustrate this point, consider the following geological situations: (a) a sedimentary basin dominated by sandstones situated within a basement of metamorphic gneisses, and (b) a large granite intrusion, the same shape as the basin above, emplaced within similar gneisses. Without independent geological information, to what extent do you think each of gravity, magnetic and seismic surveys would be able to deduce the true geological difference between these two areas?

The geometry of the boundary between contrasting rock types is an important feature which we aim to determine geophysically. This can become quite difficult in the case of horizontal boundaries, as shown in Figure 2.1 (black lines), where a uniform horizontal boundary between two layers of different density cannot be detected gravitationally.

What other geophysical technique might be suitable for detecting such a boundary?

Seismic refraction across, or reflection from boundaries between layers with different wave propagation speeds is sensitive to this kind of problem. Note, however, that there will be a gravity anomaly if there are vertical displacements on the boundary (red lines in Figure 2.1). Just in case you are reaching the conclusion that seismic techniques solve all problems in geophysics and that this makes other techniques redundant, try visualizing the relative merits of gravity and seismic surveys when the boundaries are nearly vertical. Gravity may well be more useful in such a case; moreover, you will realize that seismic techniques are generally much more expensive than other geophysical techniques. They tend to be employed in follow-up studies when interesting targets have been identified by other, cheaper techniques. This is also the approach we shall adopt in looking at the structure of the UK lithosphere, first with gravity and magnetism, and subsequently (in Section 3) with seismic methods. We shall not be considering electrical and radioactive techniques in this Block, partly because of the limitations of space, but also because there is less information available on the UK lithosphere from these methods.

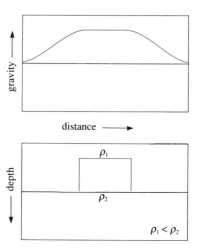

Figure 2.1   Gravity signal produced by two horizontal layers (black lines) and by a local upwards displacement of a high density layer (red lines).

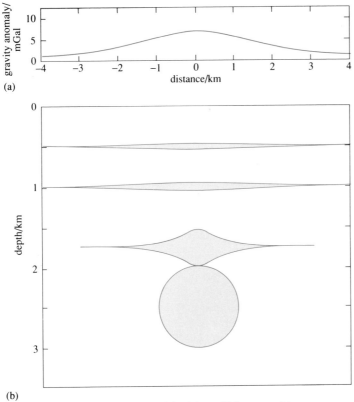

(a)

(b)

Figure 2.2 The gravity anomaly observed in (a) could be caused by any one of the four different-shaped bodies at different depths in (b). The bodies all have the same density which is 1.0×10^3 kg m^{-3} greater than the surrounding rock.

A final general point to note about geophysical surveys is that because we are attempting to deduce an unknown structure from surface measurements, there is a problem of ambiguity. This is because several possible structural interpretations (e.g. Figure 2.2) generate the same geophysical signal. No matter how precise our geophysical measurements may be, therefore, there is often no unique solution, and we need additional information in order to approach the real interpretation. This might comprise well-constrained physical property data, knowledge of geologically plausible locations and/or shapes of plausible geological structures. In some cases, if more than one geophysical technique is used to investigate an area, the range of possible interpretations becomes more limited than if only one technique is applied. So, for example, by looking at both gravity and aeromagnetic maps of Britain, we can learn a great deal more than by using either one alone.

2.2 GRAVITY AND MAGNETIC SURVEYS

You may have been wondering why the title of this Section includes the words 'potential field studies'. Well, the term **potential field** arises from the gravitational and magnetic fields of force created respectively by objects with anomalous mass and/or magnetism; these forces create the 'potential' for movement if a second object is brought within the force field of the first. (Note that there is no simple relationship between density (mass per unit volume) and magnetic properties for any particular rock—Table 2.2). The strength of the force (F) depends on an inverse square law such as:

$$F = G \frac{m_1 m_2}{r^2} \tag{2.1}$$

which is *Newton's law of gravitation*, where G is the universal gravitational constant 6.67×10^{-11} N m^2 kg^{-2}, and m_1 and m_2 are two masses separated by distance r. There is, of course, a similar inverse square relationship for magnetic force.

8

2.2.1 Some basic principles

Gravity

The force of gravity at the Earth's surface is one with which we are all familiar. You will recall that force may be defined as mass multiplied by acceleration ($F = Ma$). So, for any object at the surface of the Earth, we can replace F in equation 2.1 by mg, where g is the *acceleration due to gravity*. The mass of the object is then cancelled from both sides of the equation to yield:

$$g = \frac{GM}{R^2} \tag{2.2}$$

Here, M and R are now the mass and radius of the Earth. What this equation tells us is that if the Earth were perfectly uniform, in the sense that the mass beneath the surface varies consistently along any radius (constant M for different locations), and if it were a smooth sphere (constant R) there would be a constant value of gravitational acceleration. Of course, this is true to a first approximation, but, because the Earth is flattened slightly, g varies by about 0.5% from a mean value of 9.832 m s^{-2} at the poles to 9.780 m s^{-2} at the equator. This is why the variations of latitude between different points within a gravity survey area must be taken into account, by correcting the data, before any effects due to mass variations beneath the surface can be assessed. This is done by subtracting the **International Gravity Formula (IGF)** value of gravity, which is the predicted value of g at sea-level for any point on the Earth's surface, from the observed value. Similarly, local variations in topography (again, changes in R) must be assessed, and a series of corrections applied; eventually, we wish to reach the position where all the effects on g of varying R (equation 2.2) across the field area have been removed, leaving only the effects due to mass variations. All maps and diagrams that we shall be using have been through the necessary stages of correction for latitude, elevation, topography, density variations, etc., yielding **Bouguer gravity** values, which are values of acceleration due to gravity caused only by effects within the Earth. So the corrections that are applied to field gravity data need trouble us no further in this Course.

In order to conduct field surveys, instruments called gravimeters are used; these are very sensitive spring balances carrying a constant mass—so sensitive that they can measure differences in gravity down to 1 part in 10^8 of the Earth's gravity field. Variations in gravitational acceleration over the Earth's surface cause variations in the force acting on the mass, making the length of the spring vary. A restoring force is applied to counter-balance the effects of the gravitational force, and adjusted until the spring is returned to its original length; the magnitude of this restoring force can be read accurately from the instrument, thereby giving a value of gravitational acceleration. Gravimeters are used to measure the *difference* in gravitational acceleration between various locations. Absolute gravity is more difficult to measure, and is not needed in the context of assessing the geological structure of the lithosphere. Again, the gravity data we shall be using have all been measured and corrected with respect to some fixed datum, and have then been plotted and/or contoured.

The changes or *anomalies* in gravitational acceleration due to variations in the mass of unit volume of the lithosphere (i.e. due to density variations) are of the order of $100-1\,000 \times 10^{-6}$ m s^{-2}, (i.e. 10–100 millionths of the mean value of 9.8 m s^{-2}). So, instead of m s^{-2}, we use a more convenient unit in gravity exploration—the *milligal* (mGal)— where

$$1 \text{ mGal} = 10^{-3} \text{ cm s}^{-2} = 10^{-5} \text{ m s}^{-2} = 10 \text{ gravity units (g.u.)}$$

The Gal, named after Galileo, is 1 cm s^{-2}, which is about one thousandth of the Earth's field, so the milligal is 1 millionth of the Earth's field. Numerically, there are 10 of the gravity units you may have met in previous courses to every mGal, but g.u.s are rarely used, even in the scientific literature.

ITQ 2.2 (a) What is the difference in mGals between the mean value of gravitational acceleration at the poles and the equator of the Earth?

(b)   How many times smaller than this difference are typical anomalies due to density variations within the lithosphere, and what is their size in mGals?

(c)   How much more sensitive still are the gravimeters with which we measure the anomalies in (b)?

This exercise, although rather numerical, should have helped you to understand the importance of eliminating the effects of variations in R (equation 2.2) which, even in a small field area, often cause larger differences in g than those due to lithospheric density variations. ITQ 2.2 also demonstrates that gravimeters are capable of measuring gravity differences several orders of magnitude smaller than those typically encountered in the field. One final point: when geophysicists use the term 'gravity surveys', as you should now appreciate, they mean surveys of the variation of acceleration due to gravity (g).

Magnetics

In many ways, magnetic surveys are much more straightforward to conduct, largely because *magnetometers* are less sophisticated than gravimeters, but also because the sizes of magnetic anomalies usually lie in the range 0.1 to 10% of the Earth's magnetic field (cf. 0.001 to 0.01% for gravity). As you may recall, the Earth's field resembles, very roughly, the effect that would be produced by a dipole magnet situated close to the centre of the Earth with an axis that is slightly inclined (today by 11°) to the rotational axis. Like the intensity of magnetization about a bar magnet, the intensity of the Earth's field decreases from about 65 000 nT (nanoteslas or gammas) at the poles to about 35 000 nT at the magnetic equator.

Magnetic anomalies generated by the differences in magnetization of rocks in the lithosphere, vary from tens to thousands of nanoteslas. However, magnetic surveys become more complicated than gravity surveys when we consider anomaly sources. Firstly, for rocks to be magnetic, they must be below their *Curie temperatures*, which vary from 400 to 600 °C according to mineralogy, and contain significant amounts of the iron minerals magnetite, ilmenite or pyrrhotite.

So, how much of the lithosphere is magnetic if the geothermal gradient is a uniform 20 °C km^{-1}?

At 20 °C increase of temperature for every kilometre depth, temperatures of 400–600 °C will be encountered at 20–30 km depth.

As you know, most lithospheric geotherms are curved, so the answer may not be so simple as just illustrated, but, in general, we can say that only the uppermost parts of the lithosphere are magnetic.

The next problem is that rocks may contain different kinds of magnetism, of which two are important to us. First, there is the magnetization acquired by a rock due to its present-day position relative to the prevailing magnetic field. This is called **induced magnetization** (I) and is proportional to the strength of the ambient, or 'inducing' field (H), such that

$$I = \chi H \quad \text{[nT]} \tag{2.3}$$

where χ, the **magnetic susceptibility**, depends on the magnetic mineral content of the rock (Table 2.2). Clearly, if the rock moves or the inducing field strength changes then, respectively, the direction or strength of the induced magnetization will change accordingly. By definition, induced magnetization is parallel but in the opposite direction to the Earth's field (e.g. Figure 2.3a). Here, magnetism has been induced in the rocks beneath the surface—hence the magnetic dipole shown, which is opposite in direction to the Earth's field. Remember that the geomagnetic pole in the northern hemisphere is really the south pole of the Earth's field, which is why compass needles point their north poles in this direction (like poles repel and unlike poles attract). The lines of force created by the rocks reinforce those of the Earth's field over the south of the body, thus creating a positive anomaly; over the north of the body the opposite effect gives a negative anomaly. We return to this in Section 2.2.2.

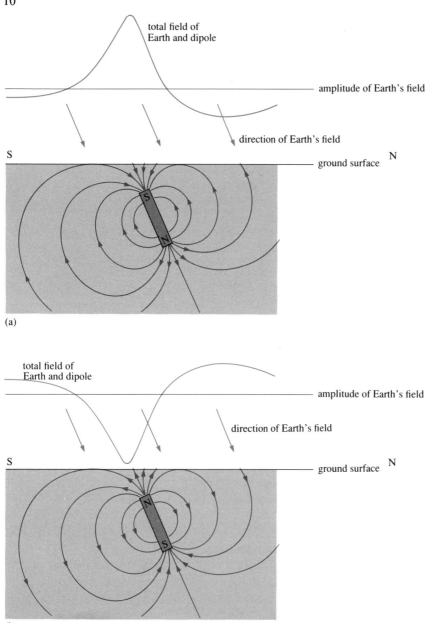

Figure 2.3 A S–N magnetic profile across a magnetic body at magnetic latitude 68° N (as in southern UK), in which (a) the magnetization is entirely induced and (b) the magnetization is entirely remanent in a direction opposite to that of the Earth's field. The measured field is a combination of the magnetic fields of the Earth and the magnetic rock.

A second type of magnetization, known as **natural remanent magnetization (NRM)** is more permanent and is acquired by rocks as they form. NRM becomes 'locked' into sediments as grains of magnetic minerals are deposited and into crystalline rocks as they cool through their Curie temperatures. Clearly, NRM must reflect the state of the Earth's field at the time the rock formed, and this is the crucial difference from induced magnetization.

As you know, the Earth's field is subject to significant changes with time (e.g. polarity reversals) and/or the continent may have moved relative to the field since the rock was formed; it follows that the NRM of a rock usually has a different direction to the present magnetic field (unless it was formed very recently). NRM of rocks can be measured in the laboratory using oriented samples of rock placed in sensitive magnetometers; this technique is applied in *palaeomagnetic studies* of both the history of the geomagnetic field and the magnetic history of the rocks. The NRM of each geological body is unique; it depends on the rock type, age and the location of formation, and so no typical values can be given as for susceptibility (Table 2.2). However, NRM can be as much as 10–100 times stronger than induced magnetization in gabbros and basalts, but in most other rock types it is equal to or more commonly less than the induced magnetization. For our purposes, then, we shall use magnetic susceptibility as a general guide to the strength of rock magnetization. NRM may supplement or reduce (depending on its direction) the intensity of induced magnetization of a geological structure, and hence be a significant factor in the interpretation of magnetic anomalies (Figure 2.3b).

Most of the data we shall consider were acquired using *aeromagnetic surveys* in which a magnetometer, such as a **proton precession magnetometer** is towed behind a fixed-wing aircraft. Such magnetometers essentially consist of a bottle of proton-rich fluid (such as water) surrounded by an electrical coil. A strong field due to current in the coil aligns the protons; when the current is removed, the rate at which the protons precess (like a spinning top or gyroscope) towards realignment with the Earth's field is measurable in terms of the strength of that field. Such magnetometers are sensitive to changes of about 0.1 nT.

How does this compare with the amplitude of typical anomalies?

This is a factor of between 100 and 10 000 smaller than anomaly amplitudes (10–10 000 nT).

So these magnetometers are quite sensitive enough to respond to typical anomalies, though the difference between instrument sensitivity and anomaly amplitude is generally not quite so impressive as for gravimeters.

The flight height of aeromagnetic surveys is determined by the horizontal resolution required and also by the local topography. As Figure 2.4 illustrates, geophysical anomalies broaden and their amplitudes decrease as the source–detector distance

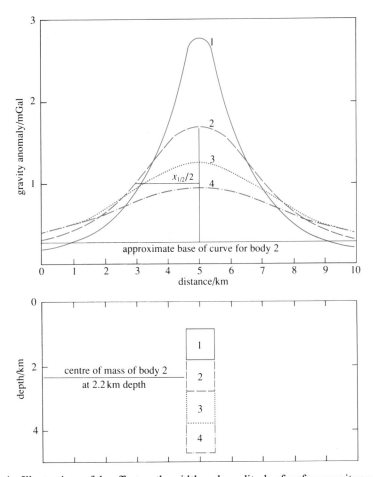

Figure 2.4 Illustrations of the effect on the width and amplitude of surface gravity anomalies of varying the depth of the body (increasing from 1 to 4) but keeping its size and density contrast constant (0.4×10^3 kg m^{-3}). The construction lines marked on the anomaly curves for body 2 indicate the use of the half width at half peak height approximation to estimate depth of burial. In this case, $x_{1/2}/2 = 2.2$ km. Note that similar features apply to magnetic anomaly source variations with similar shaped anomalies where inclination is 90°—further details in Section 2.2.2.

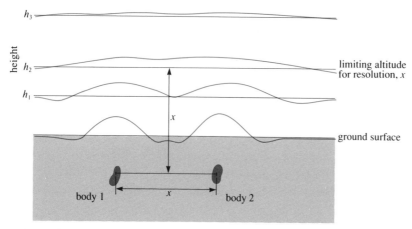

Figure 2.5 The decrease in resolution of two magnetic anomalies with increasing flight height. The magnetic effects of the two bodies are separate at h_1, but merge at h_2 (where $h_2 = x$, the distance between the bodies). At a greater height, h_3, their magnetic effects are merged and the overall amplitude of the signal is markedly decreased.

increases, so the resolution of separate anomalies decreases with increasing height (see Figure 2.5). Detailed surveys in mineral exploration, for example, require ground-based magnetic data, but for reconnaissance geophysical work where we are interested in the broad magnetic structure of the upper lithosphere, aeromagnetic surveys are ideal. However, such surveys are flown at constant height above sea-level (or above the topography), so in regions of severe topographic relief care must be taken with the interpretation of anomaly maps because they may reflect topographic as well as geological variations. (Note that airborne gravity surveys are less precise and therefore less common than aeromagnetic surveys.)

The survey is flown along a selected set of parallel lines spaced from about 100 m to several kilometers apart, depending on the size of the area of interest, heading normal to the main geological trend of the area where possible. Several control lines (so called tie lines) are flown perpendicular to and across the regular flight pattern to record second readings at the intersections as a check on consistency and diurnal variations in magnetic conditions. The field values acquired include the Earth's magnetic field and those of the magnetized (induced and NRM components) rocks. So the Earth's field is subtracted using values obtained from the **International Geomagnetic Reference Field (IGRF)**, which is a mathematical model describing the space–time characteristics of the Earth's field. Once this has been done, the values remaining are ideally a product only of rock magnetism; they are contoured to produce maps, which are then analysed and interpreted. As with gravity maps and sections, all magnetic data appearing in S339 have already been corrected.

2.2.2 Comments on interpretation

Gravity

At this stage, please find the two colour contour maps supplied with this Block, which represent the Bouguer gravity and aeromagnetic anomalies over the UK. You will find that the aeromagnetic sheet is printed in two parts with different contour intervals. This is to aid your study, because there are more prominent anomalies over northern Britain than in the south. So, for example, the northern anomalies become black with multiple contour lines if printed at the contour interval adopted for the southern section.

The numbers along the edges of these maps correspond to National Grid coordinates and represent distances in kilometres east and north of the grid origin; these are the same numbers that occur on the Geological Survey Ten Mile Maps, which you would also find useful to have available as you read on. We are fortunate to have been able to include offshore gravity data on the Bouguer anomaly map but this was not possible for the magnetic sheet for commercial reasons. The Bouguer gravity map shows variations in gravity that result from the density structure of the Earth beneath the observation area. Low Bouguer anomaly values indicate a *mass deficiency* beneath the site, and thus rocks of lower than average density, whereas high values indicate a *mass excess* associated with high density rocks. But what are the source depths of the different anomalies?

> Look again at Figure 2.4, and describe, in qualitative terms, the differences in shape and size of anomalies due to shallow and deep sources (in this case, the source volume is constant at different depths, and there is a positive density contrast of $0.4 \times 10^3 \, \text{kg m}^{-3}$).

The shape of the anomaly in each case is a single, positive peak centred over the source, but the amplitude decreases and the anomaly widens as the source becomes deeper.

There is a *rough* rule of thumb that the centre of mass of a small source lies at a maximum depth (z) approximately equal to half the width of the anomaly at half its maximum height ($x_{1/2}/2$). This is illustrated for one example in Figure 2.4; you can prove it for the rest if you wish! So, looking at the anomalies on the Bouguer map of the UK, the most prominent anomalous zones are the big negative areas, or *gravity lows* of the central Scottish Highlands and of central southern England.

> Using the half width approximation, how deep could these sources of low density rock, or maximum mass 'deficiency' be?

The most intense parts of these anomalies have total widths of a hundred kilometres or so, ranging up to 200 km across southern England. The marginal gradients are quite gentle, however, so the width at half peak height is unlikely to be greater than 100 km, in most cases markedly less. So the centres of mass responsible for these gravity lows must lie within the top 50 km of the lithosphere, and probably much shallower.

In fact, all the anomalies present on this map are due to *crustal* density or thickness variations, and we are unlikely to discriminate variations in the mantle lithosphere at this scale, though such large-scale anomalies do exist in oceanic areas as you know from Block 1A, Section 2.1.1. Nevertheless, the gradual transition from continental to oceanic lithosphere has been postulated to be responsible for the east to west overall increase in gravity across the map, and it is a feature we shall consider again later.

The half-width approximation described above is derived from formulae that relate to point sources within the Earth. But, of course, rock formations with anomalous density will have a finite width and are anything but point sources. For this reason, the depth to the centre of mass is often much less than given by the half width at half peak height $x_{1/2}/2$ approximation. For example, you will probably know that the big gravity low across southern England is caused by the low density sedimentary rocks of the Wessex Basin. In this case, the width extent of the anomaly has more to do with the extent of the basin than with its depth—for it is only a few kilometres deep. Moreover, the gentle gravity gradients around the margins of the basin are a result of gentle thinning of the sedimentary formations towards the basin edges rather than the great depth of the source. This is a good example of the need for combined geophysical and geological information in order that good constraints can be placed on lithospheric structure (see Figure 2.2). Nevertheless, all other things being equal, remember when we look at the anomaly maps in more detail that (cf. Figure 2.4) *shallow sources produce steep marginal gradients* (i.e. the slope on either side of the peak is steep) and *deep sources produce shallow marginal gradients*.

Two other factors need to be considered in making a qualitative assessment of anomalous crustal densities contributing to Bouguer gravity maps. The first of these is the density contrast between the anomalous body and surrounding rocks. The gravity data contributing to the Bouguer anomaly map of the UK were all reduced (i.e. corrected) assuming a density of $2.7 \times 10^3 \, \text{kg m}^{-3}$ down to sea-level. What this means is that positive anomalies (*gravity highs*) resulting from sources above sea-level are associated with a density greater than $2.7 \times 10^3 \, \text{kg m}^{-3}$ and vice versa for gravity lows (cf. Table 2.2). Sources below sea-level simply give anomalies related to their contrast in density compared with the surroundings.

But what will be the effect of different density contrasts on the size of a positive or a negative anomaly?

Clearly, the more the density of the source departs from that of its surroundings (i.e. the greater the density contrast), the more intense or higher in amplitude will be the anomaly. This might seem fairly obvious, but, when making judgements of this kind, we must remember that anomaly amplitude is also a function of source depth (Figure 2.4).

Finally, there is the question of how we can recognize that a particular anomaly is free from the effects of all other sources around or even beneath it. As an introduc-

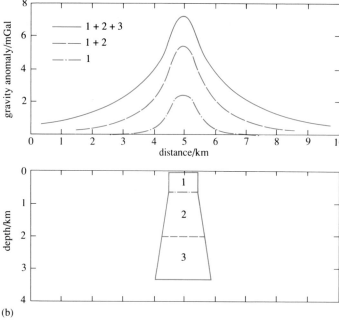

(b)

Figure 2.6 Illustration of the effect on gravity anomalies of varying the depth, extent and width of a body beneath a fixed upper surface, but again with a constant density contrast $(0.2 \times 10^3 \, \mathrm{kg \, m^{-3}})$. Similar relationships between burial depth, body size and anomaly width/amplitude hold for other types of geophysical survey.

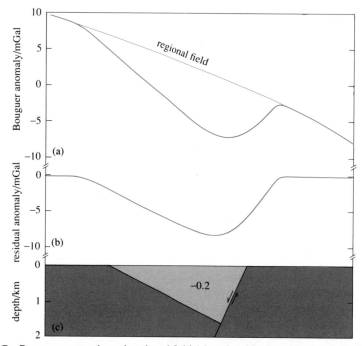

Figure 2.7 Bouguer anomaly and regional field (a) and residual gravity anomaly (b) over a half graben structure (c) filled with low-density sedimentary rocks (density contrast $-0.2 \times 10^3 \, \mathrm{kg \, m^{-3}}$). In this case, because the regional field decreases from left to right, it may be that the half graben is located over the right flank of a large, dense, basic, igneous intrusion, for example.

tion to this question, look at Figure 2.6, which shows the anomalies due to three bodies with different vertical extents but the same density contrast. Again we see that as the centre of mass deepens, so the marginal gradients become less steep. But, in this case, as we add more material, the amplitude of the anomaly increases. Suppose we wanted to produce the anomaly profile for just the lowermost part of the source, clearly we could subtract the gravity effect of the two upper blocks from the total, thus performing a crude type of **anomaly separation**. Of course, this is a very synthetic example, and you should realize that always, when interpreting geophysical anomalies, we are faced with the anomaly pattern and have to work out the most plausible source(s). Usually, anomaly separation is only undertaken when there is a small anomaly sitting on the back of some other, much larger gravity effect; this may be a larger anomaly or, perhaps, a regional trend such as the east–west increase in gravity across the UK.

So, if we want to isolate the gravity effect of a particular source in order to construct a quantitative model, the first step is to subtract the **regional field** (the sum of any regional trend, and larger anomalies) from the Bouguer anomaly to give us the **residual field**—which is that due to the source of interest. Remember that the two anomalies have markedly different widths. A simple example appears in Figure 2.7a, where the regional field decreasing from left to right, has had a negative anomaly imposed on it to give the Bouguer anomaly shown (thicker red line). The residual anomaly is obtained by interpolating the value of the regional field across the small anomaly and subtracting its value (Figure 2.7b). If we knew that the density contrast was $0.2 \times 10^3 \ \mathrm{kg \ m^{-3}}$, then a geological model could be constructed as in Figure 2.7c; in fact, this is a small half-graben structure, filled with low-density sedimentary rocks, developed on the flank of a much deeper igneous intrusion which is causing the regional gradient. We have introduced the concepts of anomaly separation and regional fields here to assist you in understanding the complexities of Bouguer gravity maps. In this Course, you will not need to carry out sophisticated anomaly separation, a technique that involves the mathematical fitting of smoothly varying surfaces to generate regional fields.

ITQ 2.3   The negative anomalies A, B and C in Figure 2.8 are due to relatively low-density granites in the Scottish Southern Uplands. (You should be able to find these anomalies on the main Bouguer anomaly map, and the three

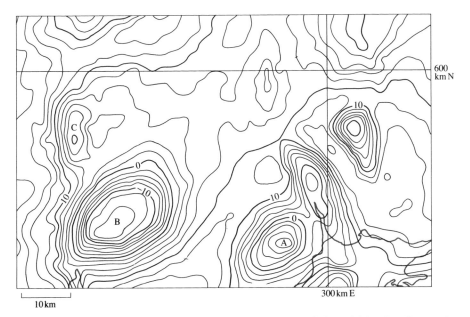

Figure 2.8   Section of the Bouguer gravity anomaly map of the British Isles (for use in ITQ 2.3) showing the gravity effects of three low-density granite intrusions (A, B, C) in the Southern Uplands of Scotland. Note that the contour interval is 2 mGal.

granites form prominent outcrops, denoted in red on the Geological Survey Ten Mile Map North Sheet. It would be good practice in the use of grid coordinates for you to match up Figure 2.8 with these two maps; note that the area is bounded by the 600 km north line and the 300 km east line) Assuming that the regional field does not vary across this area, estimate (by eye) a reasonable value for this field, and hence deduce the size of the residual anomalies due to the granites.

The differences between these three anomalies is due, in part, to the differing densities of the three intrusions. Intrusion B (the Cairnsmore of Fleet intrusion) is literally a low-density granite ($c.\ 2.6 \times 10^3\ \mathrm{kg\,m^{-3}}$), whereas A and C, respectively, include granodiorites and diorites of higher densities (2.63×10^3–$2.66 \times 10^3\ \mathrm{kg\,m^{-3}}$). All three have been modelled as occupying large volumes of the upper crust; they extend from the surface with steep sides down to about 10 km depth (e.g. Figure 2.9).

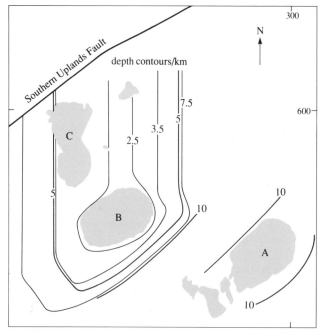

Figure 2.9 Gravity model of the Southern Uplands granite area, corresponding with Figure 2.8, and showing contours on the computed granite surface (units are kilometres below the surface).

But how are such models constructed? The most common computational approach is to assume a model, calculate the gravity effect, compare this with the observed residual anomaly, adjust the model according to the discrepancy, recalculate the gravity effect, and so on. This series of iterative steps is continued until a good agreement between the observed and calculated anomalies is achieved. A simpler approach is to compare the observed anomaly with the computed effect of certain standard shapes such as the spheres and cylinders you may have met in an earlier Course. The only shape that we need to use in this Course is the **infinite slab**, effectively a sheet which is very large in all horizontal dimensions, and which has a **gravity effect** (Δg) of:

$$\Delta g = 2\pi\, G\, \Delta\rho\, t \times 10^5\ \mathrm{mGal}, \qquad \text{or}\ \Delta g = 4.2 \times 10^{-5}\, \Delta\rho\, t \qquad (2.4)$$

where $\Delta\rho$ is the density contrast ($\mathrm{kg\,m^{-3}}$) and t is the thickness in metres. Because the slab is of 'infinite' extent horizontally, the actual depth at which it occurs does not affect the gravity anomaly it produces at the surface. What this formula allows us to do is estimate the thickness of structures that are wide and long, such as large sedimentary basins and extensive lava flows.

For example, the centre of the Wessex Basin has a gravity anomaly of $c.-35\ \mathrm{mGal}$. If the sedimentary rocks it contains have an average density of $2.5 \times 10^3\ \mathrm{kg\,m^{-3}}$ compared with $2.7 \times 10^3\ \mathrm{kg\,m^{-3}}$ in the surrounding material, what is their thickness ($G = 6.67 \times 10^{-11}\ \mathrm{N\,m^2\,kg^{-2}}$)?

The density contrast, $\Delta\rho$ is $2.7 \times 10^3 - 2.5 \times 10^3 = 0.2 \times 10^3 \, kg \, m^{-3}$; substituting in equation 2.4 gives $35 = 2\pi \, 6.67 \times 10^{-11} \times 200 \times 10^5 \, t$; so $35 = 8.382 \times 10^{-3} \, t$, so $t = 4\,176$ m. Note that the negative anomaly is due to the negative density contrast of the source compared with the surroundings. So, on this basis, we obtain $t = 4\,176$ m, and the Wessex Basin is just over 4 km deep.

While a more precise model could be obtained by computational techniques, this example serves to illustrate the value of gravity techniques in reconnaissance litho-spheric studies. Overall, of course, the interpretation of gravity anomalies is limited by the distribution of data and the ease with which anomalies can be separated. There is also the question of the inherent ambiguity in anomaly intepretation (Figure 2.2), but we hope to have demonstrated the challenge of gravity interpret-ation, which is to use other geological or geophysical constraints, and thus to determine the most appropriate model.

Magnetics

Almost all the preceding discussion about anomaly size and width variations with respect to source depth, and about anomaly separation, applies equally to the analysis of magnetic anomaly patterns. The main difference is that magnetic fields are inclined rather than being everywhere directed vertically, as with gravity. An additional difference is that gravitational forces are solely those of attraction, while in magnetics we have both attraction and repulsion to deal with. This is significant, since the dipolar nature of the magnetic field makes anomalies more complex. You should recall that magnetic inclination varies systematically from horizontal at the magnetic equator to being directed vertically downwards at the poles (see Figure 2.10 to which we return below). The relationship between inclination (i) and latitude (λ) is given by:

$$\tan i = 2 \tan \lambda \qquad (2.5)$$

So in the UK, where latitude varies from 50° N to 60° N, magnetic inclination varies from 67° to 74° and the appearance of an induced magnetic anomaly will be as in Figure 2.3a. To emphasize the point made earlier, the lines of force associated with induced magnetization reinforce those of the Earth's field strongly over the southern side of the source body, but also weakly oppose the Earth's field over the northern side. Thus, *at the latitude of the UK, there will be a strong positive anomaly south of a weak negative anomaly wherever there is a magnetic body in which the induced compo-nent of magnetism is dominant.* You should be able to see this effect locally in several places on the aeromagnetic map of the UK. There are good examples in the northern part of the Lake District (Grid Reference, GR320540), over the Somerset/Wiltshire borders (GR380150) and, on a larger scale, in the English Channel (GR330040). In these cases, the magnetization could be either induced or remanent if the dominant remanence happened to be magnetized in the direction of the Earth's present mag-netic field; the only constraint is that its *direction* in the source is roughly that of the Earth's present-day field over the UK.

> But notice that the opposite situation occurs in an east–west line of anomalies over central Devon (around GR200090 to 280090) where strong positive anomalies lie to the *north* of negative anomalies. Why might this occur?

There is a strong probability that the rocks in this area have a much stronger remanent (NRM) than induced magnetization, and that the NRM was developed in the opposite direction to the Earth's present field.

The situation is illustrated in Figure 2.3b. Notice that this type of NRM could have been acquired by the magnetic rocks forming at a low latitude but south of the magnetic equator where, by definition, the inclination is directed upwards, out of the Earth. However, geological data (Block 1A, Section 3.4.1) tell us that this is an area of Variscan magmatism—the anomalies are associated with magnetic features at the northern edge of the Variscan batholith of southwest England (which is very prominent as a series of lows on the Bouguer anomaly maps). From independent palaeomagnetic data, we know that this part of Britain was north of the equator in Variscan times, though at lower latitudes than today. Under these circumstances,

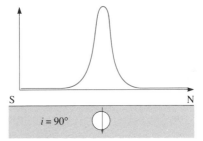

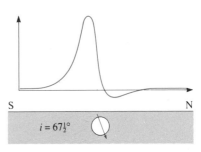

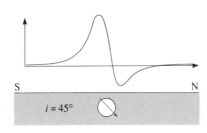

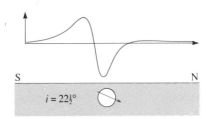

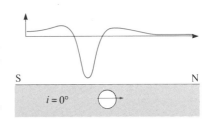

Figure 2.10 The variation of magnetic anomaly with (magnetic) latitude (i is inclination). The magnetized body is a sphere, and the anomaly shapes reflect the type of anomaly produced by either induced or remanent magnetization at each latitude. Of course, for the purposes of palaeomagnetism, rocks must carry their anomaly pattern as NRM to a different latitude; the shape of the distinctive anomaly is one way of determining palaeolatitude.

Figure 2.10 shows that the stronger anomaly will be developed on the north side of the source body (e.g. $i = 22.5°$ where there is a strong negative to the north), but, in order for this to be a positive anomaly, the Earth's field must have been reversed. So the conclusion from this analysis is that we have a source with a strong NRM, probably formed at low latitudes in the northern hemisphere under a prevailing reversed field. We hope you agree that a combined knowledge of the magnetic field and geology of central Devon has produced some interesting deductions. The next stage, were we to take this analysis further, would be to obtain information on NRM strength for the rocks of this area and to compute models of the sub-surface geology in the same way as is done for gravity.

A further difference between gravity and magnetic anomaly interpretation arises from the much greater natural variation in rock magnetism as compared with rock density. Magnetic susceptibility ranges through several orders of magnitude (Table 2.2), whereas density varies by a factor of less than two for most rocks. The great strength of some magnetic sources is the reason why we have expanded the contour intervals towards the very high and low ends of the range on the magnetic anomaly map. But notice something else: in the case of gravity, a large negative anomaly (e.g. over the Wessex Basin) just means that the rocks are a little less dense than normal. Is the same true for magnetic anomalies; do broad negative magnetic anomalies indicate less magnetism than normal in the source rocks?

> For example, how would you interpret a rather gentle negative magnetic anomaly of the type centred over Cardigan Bay, both on the mainland (GR260260) and just off the coast of central Wales?

You would be right to think that the rocks beneath this area have a below-average magnetic susceptibility. In fact, there cannot be any strongly magnetized rocks here, because, as we have seen, a complicated magnetic field with positive and negative anomalies would then result. As with gravity, there could be a *deep* source, on average opposing the Earth's present-day field, thus giving a *wide* negative anomaly. But, more likely, the rocks have a much lower magnetic susceptibility than in areas where anomaly amplitudes are greater.

Indeed, we know from independent geological and borehole data that Cardigan Bay is another deep sedimentary basin, this time containing mainly Palaeozoic sedimentary rocks of normal crustal density (see Ten Mile Map (South)). So there is no large negative gravity anomaly, but these rocks have *low magnetic susceptibility*. (You may have noticed that further offshore on the Bouguer gravity anomaly map, between the 100 and 200 km eastings lines, there is a NE–SW negative gravity anomaly; this is a Mesozoic sedimentary basin—the North Celtic Sea Basin.) So the strength of rock magnetism in the Palaeozoic strata is weaker than average, creating a *weak* negative anomaly when the IGRF is subtracted from the observed field. *So, deep sedimentary basins with relatively non-magnetic strata tend to produce weak negative magnetic anomalies and smoothly varying contours.*

> How then do we interpret stronger negative magnetic anomalies, with a larger amplitude, as seen, for example, in the English Channel?

These must be due to strongly magnetized source rocks within which the local field, on average, opposes that of the Earth's present-day field. This could be due, as we saw earlier, to reversed NRM, or due to NRM crystallized at some more southerly latitude where a strong magnetism in the opposite direction to the present geomagnetic field was acquired (Figures 2.3b and 2.10).

So the rule of thumb is that *strong positive or negative magnetic anomalies indicate a strongly magnetic source with high values of magnetic susceptibility and often a strong NRM*. We hope you can now see an important contrast with gravity, where low density simply causes negative anomalies and high density causes positive anomalies; strong magnetic anomalies depend on the direction of the magnetic field in the source.

> But what *type* of rocks will give strong magnetic anomalies?

Strongly magnetic rocks are, in general (Table 2.2), either of igneous or (less prominently) of metamorphic type: so igneous and metamorphic complexes give rise to high-amplitude magnetic anomalies, often with steep marginal gradients.

Some very clear examples occur in north and south Wales, where there are **magnetic rough zones** (regions with complex anomaly patterns having steep internal and marginal gradients) that contrast strongly with the smooth contours of Cardigan Bay (a **magnetic smooth zone**). In the Harlech Dome of north Wales, for example, several small anomalies, tens of kilometres in width, rise to values in the 500–700 nT interval compared with the 100 km wide -150 nT anomaly in Cardigan Bay. Both the Harlech Dome and the Pembrokeshire area of south Wales are characterized by a rather thin veneer of Palaeozoic sediments covering topographic highs in the sub-Palaeozoic crystalline 'basement'. Much of this basement is composed of Caledonian igneous and metamorphic rocks of various types, as you can see from the numerous small outcrops in these areas marked on the Ten Mile Map. The many magnetic sources beneath the Harlech Dome and Pembrokeshire must be carrying a strong induced (or parallel NRM) magnetization producing, overall, a complex, generally *positive* anomaly pattern with steep internal gradients—a magnetic rough zone. Any weaker negative anomalies that we might expect at this latitude (Figure 2.10b) are probably cancelled out by the effects of many strong sources. Moreover the magnetic 'roughness' of these areas is a function of the varying *directions* of NRM, some crystallized in a reversed field, as well as variations in field strength of the source rocks. *So crystalline basement highs with strongly magnetic igneous and metamorphic rocks tend to produce strong, often positive magnetic anomalies with the steep and rapidly varying gradients of magnetic rough zones.*

Although the detailed quantitative interpretation of magnetic anomalies is very complicated and subject to ambiguity, we hope you can now appreciate why magnetic methods are among the most widely used geophysical techniques. Because they are particularly rapid and cheaply-executed types of survey, magnetic methods are widely used for regional geological mapping, for reconnaissance surveying to locate possible hydrocarbon-bearing sedimentary basins, and in the search for metalliferous mineral deposits. Our objective in the next Section is to extract information on the three-dimensional coarse structure for the lithosphere using the general principles introduced above, particularly the comments about magnetic rough and smooth zones.

Summary

1   In this Section, we have briefly revised the basic principles and intrumentation involved in gravity surveys (the variation in the acceleration due to gravity) and in magnetic surveys (variations in the total magnetic field) across the Earth's surface. After appropriate correction, including subtraction of the predicted IGF and IGRF, gravity and magnetic anomalies presented in the form of maps and sections are interpreted in terms of variations in the density and strength of magnetization (induced and/or remanent) of rocks within the shallow lithosphere. Variations in density at great depth cause anomalies of greater width than occur on the maps we are studying; there are no deep ($> c.$ 30 km) magnetic sources because the Curie temperature of all rocks is exceeded at 600 °C.

2   The common unit of gravity measurement is the milligal (mGal, or 10^{-5} m s^{-2}), and since the Earth's field is almost 10 m s^{-2}, map contours in milligals are effectively parts per million of the Earth's gravity. The common unit of magnetic measurement is the nanotesla (nT), and since the strength of the Earth's magnetic field (the geomagnetic field) is almost 50 000 nT in the UK, map contours in nano-teslas are roughly parts per 50 000. Thus a 10 mGal anomaly represents a fluctuation of 0.001 % in the Earth's gravity whereas a 500 nT anomaly is a 1 % fluctuation in the Earth's magnetism.

3   A preliminary examination of the Bouguer gravity anomaly and total field magnetic maps of the UK has been used to illustrate aspects of anomaly interpret-ation. The centre of mass causing a gravity anomaly can be deduced roughly from

the half width at half peak height approximation with the proviso that most sources are broad (e.g. sedimentary basins and igneous intrusions) and do not resemble 'point' sources. In such cases, the infinite slab approximation (equation 2.4) provides a better estimate of source thickness. Another useful generalization is that, all other things (e.g. density contrast) being equal, shallow sources produce steep marginal gradients and deep sources produce shallow marginal gradients. The separation of superimposed anomalies into residual (usually small width) and regional (larger width) components is often necessary when analysing a gravity contour map.

4   Similar constraints apply to magnetic anomaly interpretation except that (a) almost all sources have inclined magnetization (Figure 2.10), and (b) there are various combinations of induced and NRM (which may have any fossilized direction) components. In general, deep sedimentary basins have rather weak negative anomalies with smoothly varying contours. Crystalline rock basement highs have strong, high amplitude positive or negative (in the UK, mostly positive) magnetic anomalies with steep and rapidly varying gradients—these are magnetic rough zones.

5   At the qualitative level, the modelling of potential fields is ambiguous (Figure 2.2) unless multiple data sets can be interpreted together. However, gravity and magnetic maps provide an important qualitative insight into lithospheric structure; in the next Section, we can now take a deeper look at the structure and history of the UK lithosphere (cf. Block 1A Section 3.4) using potential field data.

2.3   INTERPRETING THE POTENTIAL FIELD MAPS OF BRITAIN

You are now in a position to make full use of the two colour maps, introduced in the previous Sections, to look at the structural framework of Britain. Our aim will be to distinguish the contrasting geophysical signatures of areas that might represent different terranes, and also to identify the locations and approximate depth extents of igneous intrusions and sedimentary basins. To help you, we need to introduce three more 'visual aids':

1   Figure 2.11 is another version of the UK Bouguer anomaly data, processed to give a **shaded relief gravity map**. The strengths of the Bouguer anomalies are represented by apparent relief in the same way that ground elevations appear on an aerial photograph. But there is one important difference: if you have used aerial photographs in Britain, you will be accustomed to seeing the relief with illuminations from the south whereas, in Figure 2.11, the illumination is from the north. Gravity lows, for example those of the Eastern Highlands and Cornish granites, have shaded areas in the north and appear bright towards the south of what, on this map, are topographic lows. For broad structural information, many people find relief maps are more useful than colour contour maps, particularly for gravity data, and this is because the relief picks out steep **anomaly gradients**; we recommend that you use both contour and relief maps in conjunction. But first, spend a few minutes getting used to Figure 2.11 by comparing it with the colour Bouguer anomaly map.

2   In the *Colour Plate Booklet*, Plates 1.1 and 1.2, respectively, are gravity and magnetic maps of northern England and southern Scotland in which the attributes of colour contouring and relief shading are combined. A more restricted colour scale is used than on the large contour maps, but blue areas are again negative, and yellow to red areas positive with the colour intensity increasing with anomaly amplitude. The relief shading is again from the north. We include these Plates in order to focus on an area that is critical for suturing of the Iapetus ocean, though they show many other features (e.g. the granites of Figure 2.8 are clearly distinguished in the northwest corner of Plate 1.1.

3   Finally, this is the ideal point to view the first 13 minutes of the video programme: *Fragments of Britain*, which you will find on videocassette VC 271. After a brief introduction, Dr Roger Hipkin of Edinburgh University discusses the parallels between the Bouguer anomaly data of the UK and known geology using the Ten Mile Maps. His Bouguer anomaly maps are on a larger scale than yours, and they are coloured only in blue (negative anomalies) and red (positive anomalies). After a rapid survey of the geology and gravity of Britain, he then discusses the use of

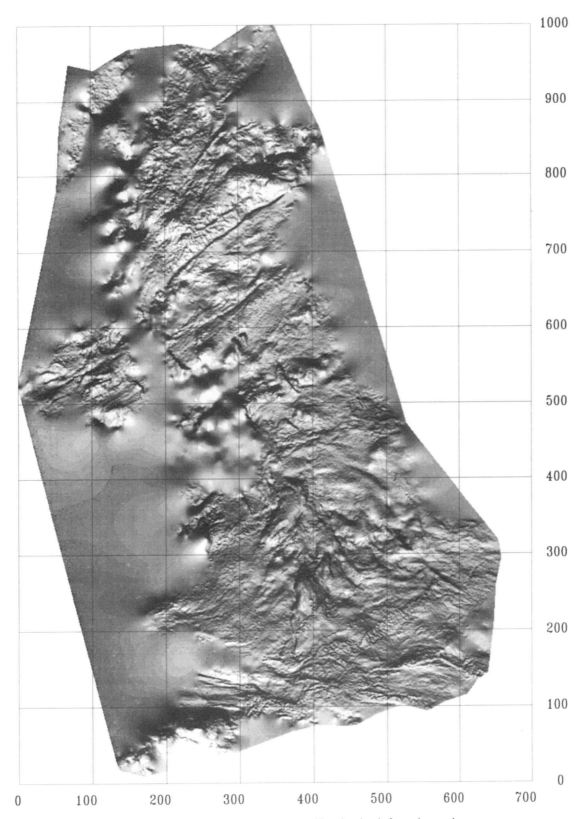

Figure 2.11 Shaded relief Bouguer gravity image of the UK; illumination is from the north.

gravity in exploring the unexposed lithosphere, and introduces the idea of **gravity provinces** which have their own distinctive signature, due to deep sources, and may thus be separate terranes. The programme is introduced by Dr Corinne Locke of Auckland University (who was a visiting lecturer at the Open University when this programme was made), and you should now view the first part of this programme, stopping when Dr Locke returns to introduce the second sequence, which is relevant to Section 3 of this Block.

2.3.1 Structural and tectonic trends

Earlier, we noted that one of the most striking characteristics of the gravity field over Britain is the overall change from negative values in the east to positive values in the west. Although the source of this effect is much debated, it is partly due to the transition from low-density continental crust to high-density oceanic crust at the western edge of the continental European plate. The North Sea also influences the shape of the gravity field across mainland Britain.

> First look back at Figure 3.20 in Block 1A and try to account for the principal features on the gravity contour map east of Britain, in the North Sea area.

Gravity highs ranging up to 50 mGal occur over the graben areas of the northern North Sea, particularly the Central Graben. This indicates a thinning of the crust in this area (cf. Block 1A, Figure 2.15c), bringing high-density mantle rocks close to the surface, and possibly also that magma was emplaced or erupted into the graben because of stretching at high strain rates. The deep sedimentary basins to the south are characterized by broad gravity lows ranging down to -30 mGal.

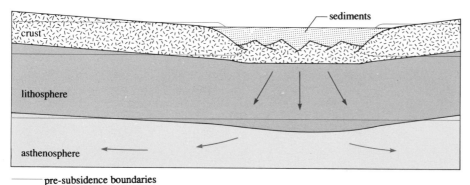

pre-subsidence boundaries

Figure 2.12 Schematic diagram (based on Block 1A, Figure 3.15) to illustrate the effect of sediment stretching and subsidence on the sub-surface and surrounding regions. Asthenospheric material moves laterally creating a peripheral bulge in the regions adjacent to those subsiding. Gravity is high over the graben itself due to magma emplacement, low on the immediate flanks due to sinking, and high in the zone over the peripheral bulge.

It is possible that extension in the North Sea basin may have caused the whole lithosphere to bend, or *flex* in an east–west direction, with regions immediately adjacent to the thinned area being pulled down, generating a mass deficiency, and therefore reducing gravity. Regional uplift further west creates a peripheral bulge more remote from the subsidence zone (cf. Figure 2.12) and may have increased the gravity field there. So the influence of North Sea subsidence provides a second possible explanation for the east–west gravity increase across Britain.

> Is there an analogous change in the magnetic field pattern across Britain?

Although the data coverage is less extensive than for gravity, the magnetic contour map shows no corresponding effect in southern Britain. But in the north there are high intensity magnetic anomalies associated with the Tertiary igneous centres from Skye south to the Antrim Plateau of Northern Ireland.

These Tertiary centres produced vast areas of lava flows and it turns out that most of these crystallized in a reversed magnetic field and carry a strong NRM opposite to the Earth's present field—there are strong negative anomalies of small width due to shallow sources in Northern Ireland. The centres from which the lavas emanated now appear as eroded intrusive complexes which have prominent signatures on both the gravity and magnetic maps. These are considered further in Section 2.3.2.

Returning to the gravity map, you may also have noticed in the North Sea area two NW–SE trending gravity highs situated at the eastern edge of the map between northings 200 and 400. The more northerly of these highs is confined almost entirely to the North Sea area, though it grazes the coast of North Yorkshire. The southern high passes through East Anglia and the English Midlands, heading northwest to an area stretching from Lancashire to the Lake District, and becoming lost in the gravity highs towards the west of mainland UK. The shaded relief map, Figure 2.11, also brings out strong NW–SE trends across eastern and central England.

> What is the size of these anomalies, and what does this suggest about the density of the source rocks as compared with mean crustal densities in this area?

The amplitude of these anomalies is not great, ranging up to a maximum of about 30 mGal above the east–west regional gradient, so the source rocks must have densities only a little above the mean.

> But what happens to the magnetic field along the trend of these gravity anomalies?

A very prominent zone of magnetic highs, ranging up to 200 nT, extends along a similar NW–SE trend roughly between northings 250 and 400 at the eastern edge of the map to northings 400 to 500 at the west coast of England.

This zone dominates the southeast corner of Plate 1.2; notice that it terminates in the southern part of the Lake District (Cumbria). You will have noticed that the gravity and magnetic highs are not entirely coincident along this zone; in particular, the magnetic highs extend slightly further north. Because the source rocks must have a strong magnetic contrast with their surroundings but a small density contrast, the magnetic map probably gives a better definition of this anomalous zone.

> What about the source rocks? Are there any clues on the Ten Mile Map; what are the principal geological trends across this area?

This is a region of late Palaeozoic (Carboniferous and Permian) to Cretaceous sedimentary rocks, which should be relatively non-magnetic and lower in density than the crustal mean. Moreover, they trend N–S to NE–SW, in places almost at right angles to the potential field anomalies. In fact, the boundary of the anomalous zone is only clearly correlated with surface geology in eastern Yorkshire and Lincolnshire, where there is a marked discordance at the edge of a Cretaceous sedimentary basin, which thickens rapidly to the east. The boundary is underlain by a postulated low-density granite at Market Weighton (GR490440) where the associated negative gravity anomaly disturbs the trend of the anomalous zone, but only on the gravity map.

So, we can now say that the sources of the NW–SE anomalous zone across eastern and central England (i) *may* have variable density, but are consistently strongly magnetic, and (ii) have little association with surface geology and must reflect buried structures at quite shallow depths. Many of the individual anomalies on both maps are symmetrical, with widths as small as 10 km suggesting maximum depths to source ($x_{1/2}/2$) of 2.5 km. The line of 5–10 km wide magnetic anomalies with steep marginal gradients across Leicestershire (GR450320 to 510290) probably reflects even shallower sources with anomaly widths almost equal to source widths (cf. Figure 2.4).

> This provides a clue to the nature of the anomaly sources. Examine the geology around GR450320, and see if you agree.

Here we find late Precambrian to Palaeozoic metasedimentary rocks, diorites, rhyolites and granites of the Charnwood Forest–South Leicestershire area. Many of these crystalline rocks would be quite capable of generating strong magnetic anomalies together with a range of gravity anomalies through their various densities (Table 2.2).

You should recall from Block 1A, Section 3.4.1, particularly Figure 3.23, that we introduced the idea of a Midlands Craton with Cadomian crystalline 'basement' of late Precambrian age. Although these rocks have been located in boreholes in the East Midlands, their extent at shallow depths was not defined until the potential field maps became available.

We have seen that the eastern part of England has a prominent NW–SE structural grain and is formed of parallel pre-Carboniferous ridges and in fact there are three of these. The first, most northerly ridge (zone 1) is confined to the North Sea (as seen on the gravity map); the second (zone 2) extends from East Anglia to the Lake District, while a third (zone 3—see aeromagnetic map) is centred on the Thames Basin–West Midlands area. Zone 3 and the southern part of zone 2 have known Cadomian basement rocks; together they comprise the Midlands Craton—further details later in this Section. Zone 3, which also extends across to Belgium and in an earlier course was called the London–Brabant massif, again is prominent on the magnetic map but has only a minor influence on gravity because of the superimposed effects of low-density sedimentary rocks in the Thames Basin overlying magnetic basement. This massif acted as a major sedimentary divide from Devonian to early or mid-Cretaceous times. The southern boundary must be overthrust at deep levels by the Variscan Front (Block 1A, Figures 3.21 and 3.23) which is coincident with the sharp gradients due to the north-south change from magnetic rough to smooth zones, particularly across south Wales. This trend is expressed on the shaded gravity relief map (Figure 2.11) but is not prominent on the gravity contour map. The mid-to-upper Palaeozoic metasediments above the thrust are apparently much less magnetic than the Cadomian basement of the Midlands Craton.

We have considered the deep structure of eastern England in some detail for the simple reason that our knowledge depends almost entirely on potential field data with some support from isolated outcrops and boreholes. As you will see shortly, most other structural and tectonic trends in the UK have a much more obvious surface expression or signature. But why does the structural grain in this essentially late Precambrian to Palaeozoic basement contrast so strongly with the NE–SW Caledonian trends that are so prominent further north?

To answer this question we must return to the three-plate model for the evolution of the Caledonides discussed in Block 1A, Section 3.4.2 (Figure 3.29). The extension of

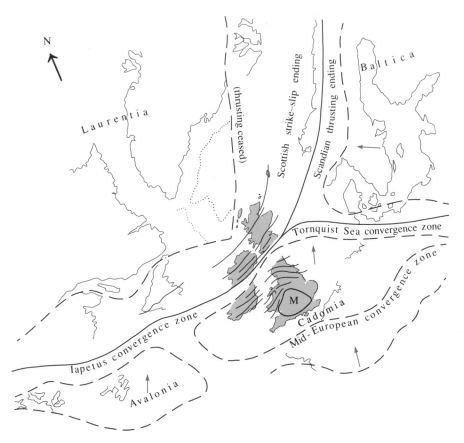

Figure 2.13 Caledonian geotectonic model for early Devonian time after collision between Baltica and Laurentia but with late Precambrian Cadomian terranes in the process of accretion. M is the Midlands Craton around which Caledonian volcaniclastics are wrapped following the trends given by the fine lines.

the Caledonian ocean (Iapetus) east into central Europe is known as the Tornquist Sea NW–SE trend. During closure, Caledonian structures were produced with this alignment in north Germany and Poland. It is envisaged that Tornquist-trending basement extends with a NW–SE grain into eastern England, but that lithosphere with the more normal NE–SW Caledonian trends occurs to the west, and is seen as magnetic lineaments in north Wales and the Irish Sea. There is even a suggestion that the structural grain in northern England is curved around the northern edge of the Midlands Craton. This is illustrated in Figure 2.13 and is expressed in the magnetic highs across the southern half of Plate 1.2. Jack Soper of Leeds University and co-workers suggest that this arcuate trend resulted, during plate convergence, from compression of Caledonian volcaniclastic rocks during the northward migration of the rigid Midlands Craton towards the embayment (shown in Block 1A, Figure 3.29, and this Block, Figure 2.13) in the northern shoreline of the Caledonian ocean, an embayment formed by the earlier suturing of Laurentia and Baltica.

Now that we have discussed many of the trends and have highlighted and explained some of the more elusive features of the potential field maps, it is your turn to make a consolidated list of the potential field features associated with major tectonic boundaries in the UK, starting with the following ITQ:

> **ITQ 2.4** Using the Bouguer gravity anomaly and total field magnetic anomaly maps, determine the regional trends, anomaly pattern and gradients associated with:
>
> (a) The Hebridean Craton
>
> (b) The Northern Caledonides
>
> (c) The Southern Caledonides
>
> (d) The Variscan Orogenic Belt
>
> (e) The Tertiary Igneous Province
>
> To do this, complete Table 2.3 overleaf and use Figure 2.14 for guidance.

We now need to amplify some of the points raised by ITQ 2.4.

(a) *The Hebridean craton* The high-amplitude positive gravity anomalies are directly related to the high densities of old, high-pressure metamorphic gneisses that have been exhumed from deep levels (more details in Block 5). A prominent fault—the Outer Isles Thrust—runs along the east coast of the Outer Hebrides and is coincident with steep gravity gradients. The fault forms the western margin of the Mesozoic Minches sedimentary basin, a basin that effectively separates the high density Lewisian outcrops of the Outer Hebrides from those of mainland Scotland (see Block 1A, Figure 3.20). The juxtaposition of Lewisian with low-density sediments across the fault is the cause of the prominent gravity anomaly. The magnetic anomalies over the mainland Lewisian are probably caused by Precambrian mafic dykes that are particularly abundant in this area (the Scourie Dyke swarm); the strong magnetic effects of the Tertiary dykes intensify to the south and west.

(b) *The Northern Caledonides* The NE–SW Caledonian trend is obvious on both contour maps and Figure 2.11. But what about the magnitude of the potential field values in different fault-bounded provinces?

> Take the gravity gradient across the Highland Boundary Fault, for example. What does this suggest about the density variations across the fault?

Gravity increases quite dramatically across the fault from NW to SE, implying that the crustal section through the Midland Valley is *more* dense than the equivalent thickness of Moine and Dalradian north of the fault.

If you use the Ten Mile Map together with the gravity map to compare the signatures over the Moine and Dalradian adjacent to their boundary between GR300760 and GR220730 you should see that the Moine (to the north) has an even lower density than the Dalradian. Although the Great Glen Fault disturbs the anomaly pattern, the potential field maps do indicate that the whole of northern

Table 2.3 Potential field characteristics in Britain (for use with ITQ 2.4)

Tectonic trend		Features	Orientation	Gravity expression	Magnetic expression
(a)	Hebridean Craton	gneisses of Outer Isles and NW Scotland	NE–SW		
(b)	Northern Caledonides	Great Glen Fault	NE–SW		
		Highland Boundary Fault	NE–SW		
		Southern Uplands Fault	NE–SW		
(c)	Southern Caledonides	Church Stretton Fault Zone	NE–SW		
		margins of north Celtic Sea Basin	NE–SW		
		Malvern Fault	N–S		
		E England Tornquist Trend and Pennine Fault System	NW–SE		
(d)	Variscan Orogenic Belt	Variscan Front and trends in S/SW England	W–E		
(e)	Tertiary Igneous Province	trends formed by igneous centres and Tertiary dykes	NW–SE		

27

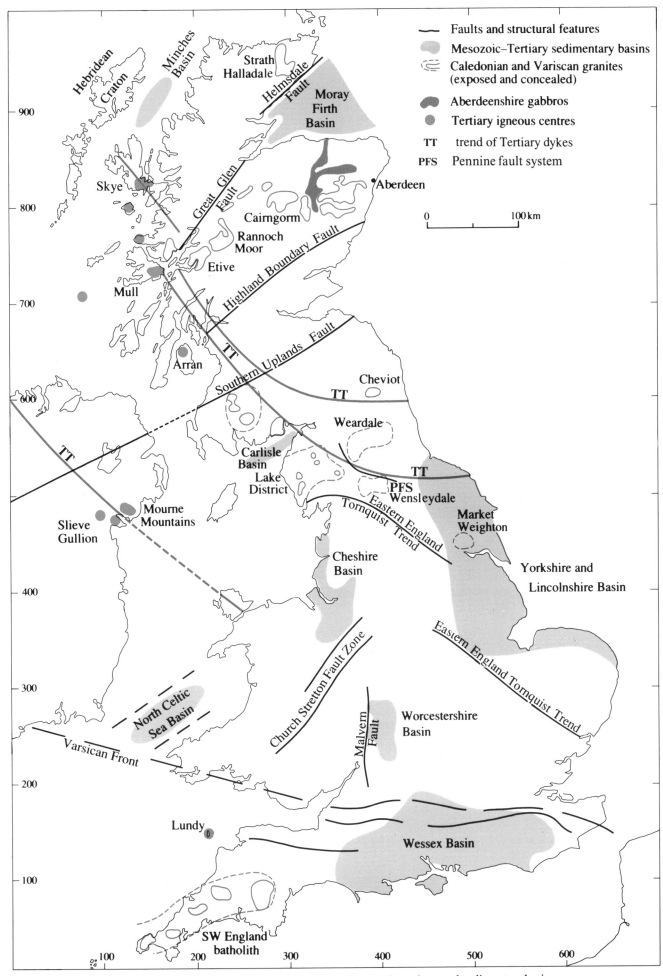

Figure 2.14 Map of Britain showing the major structural trends, igneous intrusions and sedimentary basins.

Scotland can be regarded as a unit, looking like a single terrane in tectonic terms (further details in Block 4).

In contrast, the Midland Valley (which we shall consider in Block 2) is quite distinctive geophysically; it is a region of higher Bouguer gravity and complex magnetic anomalies both along its bounding faults and over the valley itself. These complex and variable magnetic anomalies must result from shallow sources, in this case mainly due to outcropping and shallowly buried Carboniferous mafic lavas and sills. The gravity structure of the Midland Valley suggests that the low-density 'cover', mainly the exposed, undeformed Upper Palaeozoic sedimentary sequence, must be thin relative to the Moine/Dalradian further north—and this is consistent with the evidence for tectonic thickening of the metamorphic sequence north of the Highland Boundary (Block 4). We might therefore expect to find shallower high density basement beneath the Midland Valley than further north: perhaps, in keeping with the idea that the Midland Valley is a separate terrane, this area is not a simple rift valley (more discussion later and in Block 2).

As you know from Block 1A, Section 3.4.2, the Southern Uplands Fault marks another major tectonic break in the Caledonides.

> Bearing in mind our conclusions about crustal structure north of the fault, how might you explain the decrease in gravity to the south?

The lower values of Bouguer gravity in the Southern Uplands are in accord with the greater thicknesses of Ordovician and Silurian low-density rocks in the tectonically thickened accretionary prism (Block 1A Figure 3.26).

The distinctive linear magnetic and gravity trends associated with the Southern Uplands Fault are prominent in the northwest corner of Plates 1.1 and 1.2. The magnetic anomaly is most pronounced over the early Ordovician Ballantrae ophiolite (GR210580), and from the overall linear anomaly pattern it is inferred that such rocks are present at depth along the fault line from the North Sea (GR430700) across to Northern Ireland. Further south, beneath the Southern Uplands, is a broad ENE-trending magnetic high (e.g. at GR250550) of unknown origin, though its large width indicates a source beneath the Lower Palaeozoic turbidites which could be subducted oceanic lithosphere 'frozen' into position (cf. Block 1A Figure 3.27b). Other, more localized potential field anomalies in the Southern Uplands and elsewhere in the Northern Caledonides, due to igneous intrusions and sedimentary basins, will be considered in subsequent sections.

(c) *The Southern Caledonides* Moving southwards into northern England, there is no obvious change either in the overall magnetic or gravity signatures though there are intense lows over the Weardale Granite (GR400540) (Figure 2.14 and Section 2.3.2). However, a fine ENE–WSW magnetic lineament is brought out in shaded relief (Plate 1.2—it runs from the coast of Northumberland across to the northern boundary of the Solway Firth).

> To what geological feature might this magnetic lineament be related? Look at the Ten Mile Map around GR350580.

The relief map seems to be picking up a mafic dyke that crosses northern England.

Although this anomaly is actually related to Permo-Carboniferous mafic dykes, it happens to correspond well with the postulated surface location of the Iapetus suture. As you can see from Plates 1.1 and 1.2, there is no significant potential field contrast across this suture *other than* the transition from arcuate (south) to linear (north) magnetic anomalies.

On Plate 1.1, at the western edge of the Weardale Granite gravity low, there is a NW–SE gravity lineament associated with the Pennine fault system (Figure 2.14), followed by the N–S elongate low over the Permo-Triassic Vale of Eden (GR360520). Further west still, gravity increases across the Lake District in accord with the E–W regional gradient, but this is punctured by a central gravity trough corresponding to a series of low-density granite intrusions beneath the Lake District, a granite zone that extends right across northern England and to the edge of the Irish Sea. There is a sharp arcuate magnetic anomaly in the northern Lake District (Plate 1.2) which also extends, in a more subdued form (deeper sources), towards the Isle of Man.

> How do you account geologically for this arcuate anomaly in the northern Lake District?

This anomaly is associated with andesite lavas, in fact the Eycott Volcanic Group, which consists of significant lava flows containing magnetite—as opposed to the later pyroclastic tuffs of the Borrowdale Volcanic Series—and so produces prominent magnetic anomalies.

Returning to the contour maps, further south (as discussed earlier), we have the NW–SE Tornquist Trends of eastern England and the normal Caledonian NE–SW trends across western England, north Wales and the Irish Sea. You should have noticed, in completing Table 2.3, that the two trends are roughly symmetrical about the N–S Malvern Fault line (Figure 2.14), which clearly is responsible for important potential field anomalies on both maps. This fault line has had a long and complex structural history involving several phases of uplift exposing Cadomian basement at the surface. A recent proposal is that the lineament may have originated as a lithospheric suture in the late Precambrian, separating areas that exhibit crustal differences in stratigraphic, magmatic and structural histories. The Midlands Craton might therefore be composed of two originally separate terranes, east and west of the Malvern Fault line.

Although we observe that Cadomian basement extends from Anglesey in the west, beneath Wales and the Midlands to East Anglia in the east, we do not know where its northern limit lies. However, there is no geological evidence for the occurrence of Cadomian basement beneath northern England and it is believed that the Midlands Craton must have terminated before reaching south Yorkshire and Lancashire (as indicated in Block 1A, Figure 3.23, and Block 1B, Figure 2.13). In that case, post-Cadomian, Caledonian volcaniclastic rocks draped around the margin of this craton would be responsible for the northernmost belts of magnetic anomalies that appear to the south of Plate 1.2. The effects of igneous intrusions on these anomaly patterns will be discussed in Section 2.3.2.

(d) *Variscan Orogenic Belt*   Gravity and magnetic anomalies across the Variscan terrane of southern England and Wales are generally rather subdued in comparison with those of the Caledonides. For example, gravity gradients associated with the Variscan Front and faults further south (marked on Figure 2.14) are not conspicuous on the contour map, though they are brought out in shaded relief (Figure 2.11). This is partly due to the more recent development of the Wessex Basin, with a gravity signature that dominates the contour map in southern Britain, but the lack of a strong gravity contrast across the Variscan Front tends to confirm that this terrane was thrust across Britain along a rather low-angle thrust (cf. Block 1A Figure 3.22) rather than docking along a mainly strike-slip zone, which characterizes many boundaries further north. There is, of course, the strong negative Bouguer gravity effect of the southwest England batholith with the prominent reversed NRM magnetic anomalies (described in Section 2.2.2) wrapped around its northern margin (GR190090 to GR290090). If you locate the position of these anomalies on the Ten Mile Map you will find ample evidence of Devonian basalts in this area (labelled 49). It is possible that the presence of such lavas, perhaps upturned and subject to contact metamorphism along the margin of the batholith, which produced magnetic minerals, is causing this anomaly. However, such a source remains to be proved, and an alternative suggestion is that there is strong remanent magnetization in concealed dolerite dykes, again subject to thermal metamorphism.

> What about the Lizard ophiolite (around GR170020); how do you interpret the potential field anomalies associated with this area?

There are strong gravity gradients across the southeast margin of the granite batholith, but there is no specific gravity anomaly. However, there is a small, rather sharp magnetic anomaly. These features imply that there are shallow magnetic sources but no great thickness of high density ultrabasic rocks.

You will recall from Block 1A, Section 3.4.1 that the Lizard ophiolite is thought to have been emplaced by another north-directed Variscan thrust sheet, so the potential field evidence suggests that we may be seeing only the front end of a thrust sheet. Notice, however, that gravity is high all along the coast of south Cornwall, and there is a suggestion of an E–W gravity ridge extending east to GR390030. Notice, too, that this coincides with a magnetic trough—an intense negative magnetic anomaly—with sharp positive zones to the south. This line, between the Lizard and c. 40 km south of Dorset, is thought to mark the continuation of the ophiolite-bearing thrust.

So the Variscan of southern Britain is characterized by various thrusts. The associated deformation, which extends north to the Variscan Front, forms structures characteristic of thin sheets of material that have undergone tectonic stress—known as **thin-skinned tectonics**—such structures will be described in detail from modern orogenic belts in Block 4. The final point to note about the Variscan potential field trends is the rather sharp boundary of the magnetic highs of the Midlands Craton immediately north of the Variscan Front. Surely the Cadomian craton must have been overthrust from the south, so we would expect magnetic basement *beneath* the Variscan thrust sheet? There is a suggestion that magnetic basement does indeed become deeper further south of the Variscan Front beneath southeast England (e.g. around GR490130) but the lack of 'deep' magnetic anomalies elsewhere is surprising. These observations suggest that the Variscan Orogenic Belt was thrust across a rather variable topography and came to a halt against a topographic ridge, a positive basement feature, which we now see reflected in the south Wales–London area magnetic anomaly line (see Figure 2.15).

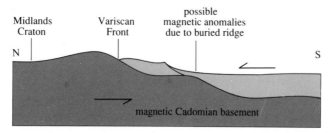

Figure 2.15 Simplified version of Block 1A, Figure 3.22, to illustrate the suggestion that the Variscan mobile terrane was pushed across southern Britain until it met a topographic ridge. The weak, but variable magnetic anomalies south of the Variscan Front suggest that the topography of the Cadomian basement beneath the thrust is also variable in height.

(e) *The Tertiary igneous province* There are three main igneous geological components and potential field anomalies resulting from Tertiary extension across western Britain: (i) the igneous centres, (ii) dykes and dyke swarms, and (iii) extensive basalt lava flows. Figure 2.16 shows the distribution of (i) and (ii), which have prominent expressions, particularly on the magnetic contour map.

Leaving aside the Tertiary intrusive complexes (see Section 2.3.2), the dyke swarms can be traced considerable distances from the centres with which they are associated (Skye, Mull, Arran and the Slieve Gullion–Mourne Mountains area). Although not obvious from the magnetic contour map, even individual dykes are traceable using magnetic relief techniques. Plate 1.2, for example, shows the NW–SE dyke trend across the Southern Uplands and northern England. The southernmost dyke–the Cleveland–Armathwaite dyke—is seen in the village of Armathwaite in eastern Cumbria (GR340550) and cuts right across England to emerge in the Cleveland area of North Yorkshire (GR500480).

To the south of Figure 2.16, the Slieve Gullion—Mourne Mountains dyke swarm cuts across the Irish Sea, where it can be traced as a linear feature on the magnetic contour map, and emerges as basalt dykes in western Anglesey. There is one other Tertiary centre further south still, at Lundy Island in the Bristol Channel (GR215145). Although its presence as an igneous centre is expressed on both

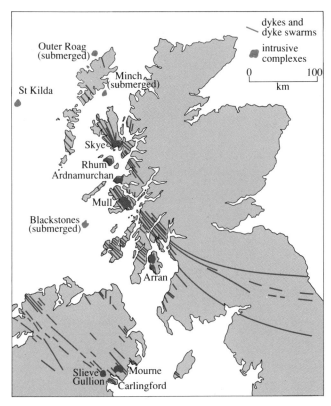

Figure 2.16 Distribution of major Tertiary igneous dykes, dyke swarms and intrusive centres in Scotland, Ireland and northern England.

potential field maps, it did not develop a major dyke swarm like the large centres further north. Nevertheless, it is likely that the presence of a Tertiary centre so far south in Britain is related to activity on a zone of crustal weakness, associated with NW–SE tear faults that cut the island.

> Finally, what about the Tertiary lavas? Where are the main Tertiary basalt lava fields on land in Britain, and what is their potential field signature?

There are three main lava fields in northern Skye, Mull and the Antrim plateau of northwest Ireland. Although these do not have a significant gravity expression, they produce some of the most intense magnetic rough zones found in Britain. However, many small width, intense negative magnetic anomalies can be resolved.

Earlier, we noted that these lava flows crystallized in a reversed field and carry a strong NRM opposite to the Earth's present field. Perhaps you can now understand more clearly why we have arrived at this conclusion; these lava sequences are thin on a lithospheric scale and produce shallow magnetic anomaly sources with no gravity effect, in strong contrast to the vertically extensive intrusive complexes that we shall examine in the next Section.

2.3.2 Igneous intrusions and intrusive complexes

Now that we have examined the overall tectonic framework of Britain using potential field maps the remaining pieces of the jigsaw fall into place quite easily. First, we shall consider the information that can be derived, using gravity and magnetic techniques, about the intrusive activity that has occurred during each of the three main tectonic episodes affecting Britain.

Table 2.4 Potential field characteristics of some typical intrusions and intrusive complexes in Britain (for use with ITQ 2.5)

Tectonic 'age'		Intrusion or complex	Gravity anomaly: pattern and amplitude	Magnetic anomaly: pattern and amplitude
(a)	Northern Caledonides	Strath Halladale		
		Cairngorm-Aberdeen		
		Aberdeenshire Gabbros		
		Etive–Rannoch Moor		
(b)	Southern Caledonides	Cheviot		
		Weardale—Lake District		
		Wensleydale		
		Market Weighton		
(c)	Variscan	SW England batholith		
(d)	Tertiary	Skye		
		Mull		
		Lundy		

ITQ 2.5 Several major intrusions and intrusive complexes are located in Figure 2.14. Using the Bouguer gravity and total field magnetic anomaly maps, describe briefly the effects of these geological features. To do this, complete Table 2.4 and use Figure 2.14 (p. 27) for guidance, together with the Ten Mile Map to locate the positions of the Tertiary intrusive complexes in Skye and Mull.

As with tectonic trends, we shall now amplify some of the points raised by ITQ 2.5.

(a) *Northern Caledonian intrusions* Apart from the Aberdeenshire gabbros, all the intrusions in this area, and indeed most of the rest in Table 2.4, are marked in ubiquitous red on the Ten Mile Map and labelled 34: granite, syenite, granophyre and allied types. Of course, very little of the material exposed is granite (in the strict sense), though granodiorite and diorite are common components of these intrusions. The detailed mineralogy and geochemistry of Caledonian intrusions will be considered in Blocks 3 and 4; all you need to know here is that these granites (in the broad sense) have densities in the range 2.55×10^3–$2.65 \times 10^3 \, \text{kg m}^{-3}$, which are lower than the host Moine and Dalradian metasediments (2.65×10^3–$2.70 \times 10^3 \, \text{kg m}^{-3}$). So, at first sight, it is surprising that Strath Halladale has no significant gravity anomaly, whereas the Etive–Rannoch Moor and Cairngorm–Aberdeen intrusions, which cut similar host rocks, have major negative anomalies. (You can see these features in more detail on the Tay–Forth geological sheet, which has grid markings down the side; this is the area covered at Summer School, where the geology will be considered in more detail.)

What do you think this might tell us about either the deep structure or the relative densities of these intrusions?

Granite intrusions with large negative gravity anomalies, representing a significant mass deficiency, must either have a much larger volume or a greater density contrast with their host rocks than those with little or no anomaly.

Thus, despite the apparently similar size of these intrusions at outcrop level, gravity data reveal that their deep structure and/or densities are very different. In fact, detailed studies of these and many more granite intrusions in the Northern Caledonides than we have time to consider have revealed that granites of the Strath Halladale type do have smaller volumes at depth *and* higher densities than the granites we have considered further south.

There are many types of Northern Caledonian intrusive complexes, and we have chosen representatives of the two most extreme types. Those emplaced *early* in the Caledonian orogeny (e.g. Strath Halladale, dated at 650 Ma) are strongly deformed, higher density, often more dioritic intrusions of *limited three-dimensional volume*. Those emplaced *at the end* of the Caledonian orogeny (e.g. Etive–Rannoch Moor and Cairngorm–Aberdeen, dated at 400–410 Ma) are undeformed, low density, often more granitic intrusions *occupying large crustal volumes*.

Notice also from your completed version of Table 2.4 (Table A2), that the two types of intrusion also contrast magnetically, with a lack of any prominent effect over Strath Halladale, but quite complex variable anomalies over most of the younger intrusions further south. Of course, granite intrusions themselves are not usually magnetic (Table 2.2), rarely containing a high percentage of iron minerals, so why are these anomalies so clearly associated with such intrusions? There are two probable reasons for this magnetic anomaly pattern; first there is a metamorphic aureole effect whereby metasediments are baked, forming magnetic minerals, and magnetized to form annular magnetic sources around the walls of the intrusion—we shall examine this process in relation to the Shap granite a little later. Second, analysis of the overall magnetic effect has revealed the presence of *deep* sources, possibly resulting from the interaction of rising magma with the basement during emplacement. To appreciate the nature of this process, first it is useful to estimate the depth, or thickness of these intrusions. As you know from the gravity contour map, the Cairngorm intrusion (GR300800) forms the most intense negative Bouguer anomaly in Britain. It also has a positive magnetic anomaly, both over the intrusion itself (deep source) and intensifying around its edges (shallow annular contact metamorphic sources).

ITQ 2.6 Just how thick is the Cairngorm granite intrusion? Use a density contrast of $0.1 \times 10^3 \, \text{kg m}^{-3}$ and the observed negative Bouguer anomaly (60 mGal maximum) to estimate this thickness using the infinite slab approximation (equation 2.4). (Note: $G = 6.67 \times 10^{-11} \, \text{N m}^2 \, \text{kg}^{-2}$.)

In one sense, this should be a minimum thickness because of the infinite slab approximation used, but in another sense, it should be a maximum since the regional field around Cairngorm is negative and the anomaly due to the intrusion alone is less than 60 mGal. Figure 2.17a gives a more detailed picture, using computed contours,

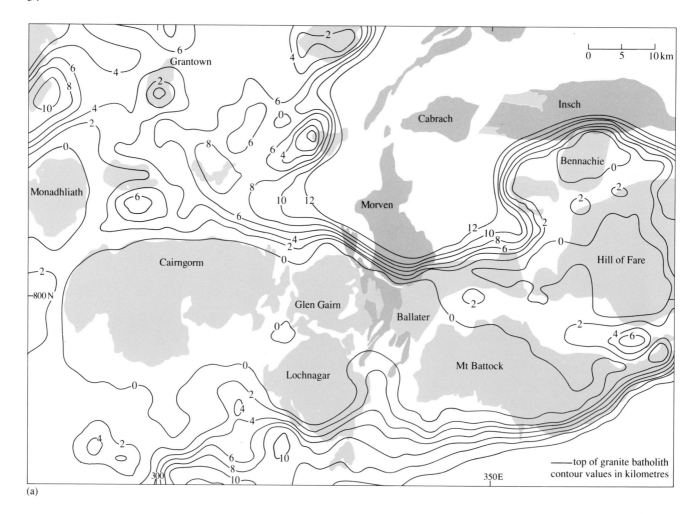

(a)

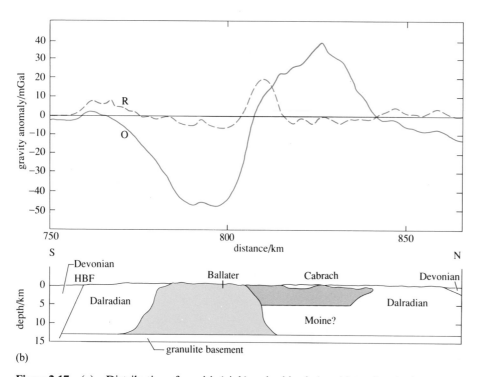

(b)

Figure 2.17 (a) Distribution of granitic (pink) and gabbroic (grey) intrusions in the eastern Highlands of Scotland, together with computer-generated contours on the upper surface of the granite bodies.

(b) Section south–north through the area shown in (a) along the 335 km east grid line showing the observed gravity (O) and the difference between the observed and calculated gravity anomalies (R). The largest difference occurs at the junction between the granite and gabbro as would be expected, since the large density contrast here is difficult to model.

of the sub-surface shape of the Cairngorm–Aberdeen granite intrusions. Notice that where the edges of the batholith are steep, along the southeast and northeast margins, the surface plunges rapidly down to 12 km; this analysis produced a best fit between observed and calculated gravity anomalies *if the base of the granite batholith is placed at 13 km depth* (Figure 2.17b) a little less than estimated in ITQ 2.6. So, to conclude our analysis of the potential field anomalies over these granites, the deeper magnetic sources must lie below about 13 km depth and probably above about 20 km depth (the approximate depth of the Curie temperature—see Section 2.2.1). It is through this region of the crust that the granite magmas must have risen, causing high-temperature metamorphism and producing magnetic sources (further details below) on route to their emplacement in what is now the uppermost 13 km of the crust.

Where the Cairngorm–Aberdeen granite intrusions take the form of outward-dipping bodies that widen with depth, the adjacent Aberdeenshire gabbros are best modelled in terms of steep-walled, but inward-dipping bodies (see Figure 2.17b). In this case, the positive density contrast is much greater 0.2×10^3–$0.3 \times 10^3\ \mathrm{kg\ m}^{-3}$, so the thickness of the source producing a $+50\ \mathrm{mGal}$ anomaly is only 5 to 7 km.

> Why do you think the magnetic gradients are so steep over the margins of these basic intrusions?

This is because basic rocks have a higher magnetic susceptibility than granites (Table 2.2), so the sources of magnetism lie *within* the modelled body, and because the source is relatively shallow but steep-sided.

So the Aberdeenshire gabbros are steep-sided, dense magnetic slabs some 5–10 km wide and thick; they were emplaced about 500 Ma ago and were affected by the late stages of Dalradian metamorphism (further details and significance in Block 4).

(b) *Midland Valley* Although we did not consider this region separately in ITQ 2.5, in Section 2.3.1 we noted that there are some prominent potential field anomalies in the Midland Valley. In view of its importance in Block 2, it is worth taking a brief look at these anomalies. Figure 2.18 provides a detailed picture of Midland Valley geology and potential field anomalies. There are four distinct gravity anomalies at Arran, Bathgate, Stonehaven and Hamilton, which you should identify. The first three are positive anomalies, and the last is negative. The simplified total field magnetic anomaly map of the area (Figure 2.18c) features two main types of anomaly: (i) complex, variable anomalies already ascribed to shallow Carboniferous sills and lavas (Section 2.3.1), and (ii) broad, smooth anomalies associated with the gravity highs at Arran, Bathgate and Stonehaven.

> Based on our analysis of anomalies north of the Highland Boundary Fault, and ignoring information on the Ten Mile Map for the moment, to what types of geological source would you attribute these four anomalous areas?

The source beneath Hamilton could be a granite intrusion or a sedimentary basin, though the circular anomaly and presence of other granites in the area indicate that a granite is more likely. The other three anomalies are much more likely to be basic intrusions.

Notice on the Ten Mile Map that none of these intrusions has a clear surface geological expression, except perhaps for the Arran anomaly which is centred over a Tertiary granite! This apparently paradoxical situation of an outcropping granite, situated in a region with the potential field signature of a basic intrusion, is common to other Tertiary centres as we shall see later. The other three Midland Valley intrusions have no such surface geological expressions; the Hamilton anomaly is probably due to a Caledonian granite intrusion while those at Bathgate and Stonehaven may well result from Carboniferous basic bodies. If these suppositions are correct, younger Carboniferous strata have covered the Hamilton intrusion, while the other two may have been emplaced within strata of this age without reaching the surface.

(c) *Southern Caledonian intrusions* The prominent gravity lows associated with granite intrusions in the west of the Southern Uplands (Figures 2.8, 2.9 and Plate

36

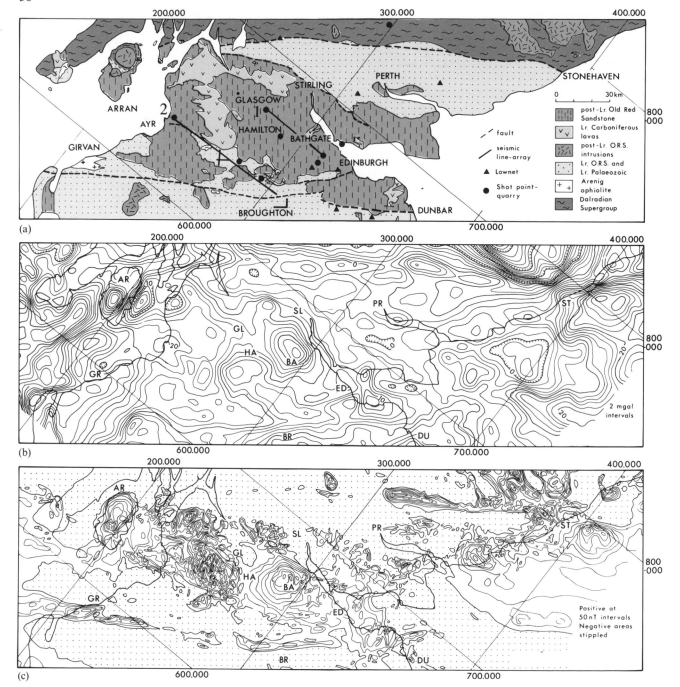

Figure 2.18 (a) Simplified geological map of the Midland Valley of Scotland with seismic
lines and stations to be discussed in Section 3.1.3;
(b) Bouguer anomaly map with place names abbreviated from (a);
(c) aeromagnetic map with negative contours omitted.

1.1) were the subject of ITQ 2.3. Similar buried granites have been located by
potential field methods further east, while at a similar latitude (GR395620), the
20 km wide anomaly over the Cheviot granite demonstrates that this intrusion is
probably quite extensive at depth with outward-dipping margins. A simplified
cross-section through the Cheviot granite (Figure 2.19) shows that this dip is quite
steep.

> What about the annular magnetic anomaly at Cheviot (Plate 1.2); to what
> geological source is this ascribed in Figure 2.19?

The source appears to be a marginal facies of the granite, beneath the two magnetic
anomaly peaks. In a fascinating study of this intrusion, M. K. Lee of the British
Geological Survey found a narrow zone of high susceptibility rocks in the marginal
facies of the Cheviot granite, as well as metamorphosed andesite lavas immediately
adjacent to the contact.

A similar situation exists at Shap in the eastern Lake District (GR355510), and you should locate the small gravity low over Shap on Plate 1.1 and the magnetic high on Plate 1.2. The sub-surface shape of the granite down to *c.* 4 km is easily modelled using gravity data (Figure 2.20a), but there is more of a problem with the magnetic anomaly (Figure 2.20b), which includes a strong positive anomaly over the intrusion itself with a weaker negative anomaly to the north.

Given that these granites were emplaced 400 Ma ago when according to palaeomagnetic data, Britain was just south of the equator, do you think the anomaly at Shap is due to induced or remanent magnetization?

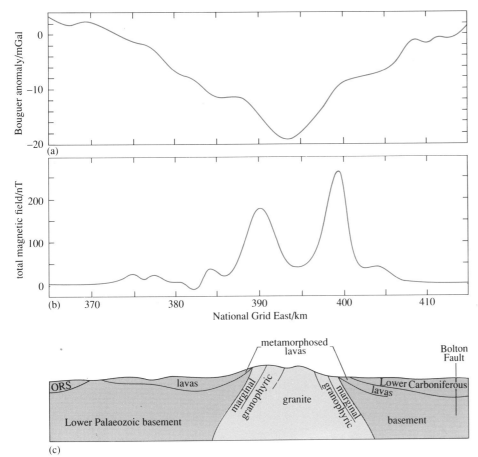

Figure 2.19 Relationship between geophysical anomalies and geology along an east–west section through the Cheviot granite along northing 620. The magnetic susceptibility of the marginal facies was modelled as 2×10^{-3} compared with 0.6×10^{-3} in the granite body.

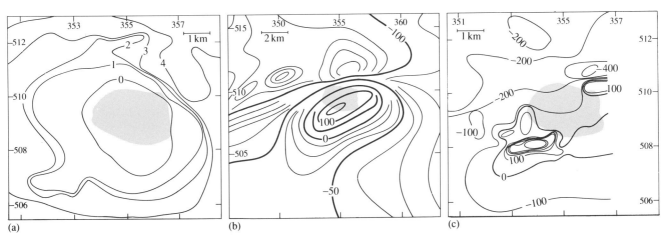

Figure 2.20 (a) Contour map showing the depth to the roof of the Shap granite based on gravity modelling.
(b) Aeromagnetic contours in the Shap granite area with major contours at 50 nT intervals.
(c) Ground-based magnetic map of the granite area with contours at 100 nT intervals.

From Figures 2.3 and 2.10, it is clear that this must be induced magnetization since Britain now has a magnetic inclination of $c.\ 68°$. (Note that remanent magnetization due to a reversed field at high latitudes in the southern hemisphere is an alternative but less likely possibility.) Indeed, the granite itself has quite a high susceptibility, measured as 8.5×10^{-3} compared with 2.8×10^{-3} in normal, unmetamorphosed Borrowdale Volcanics that form the envelope around the north of the intrusion. So the granite itself is quite capable of producing a significant anomaly. However, a more detailed ground-based magnetic survey (Figure 2.20c) has revealed that there are also two zones of strong magnetization in the Borrowdale Volcanics immediately adjacent to the northeast and southwest of the Shap granite. Measured susceptibilities in these regions range from 18.3 to 83×10^{-3}, 1 m and 20 m, respectively, from the granite contact. Together with the anomaly due to the granite itself, these small, highly magnetic zones are thought to contribute to the overall aeromagnetic anomaly which is smoothed because of the flight height (in this case 300 m above the topography). A mineralogical solution has been found in that the basaltic andesites of these two zones have been strongly hydrothermally metamorphosed in the contact aureole, producing biotite, which replaces pyroxene. Adjacent to the granite, in places, biotite has then broken down by the following dehydration reaction:

$$\text{biotite} \rightarrow \text{K feldspar} + \text{magnetite} + \text{water}$$

The appearance of magnetite where there are iron-rich rocks in contact metamorphic aureoles probably explains the occurrence of annular magnetic anomalies around some granite bodies.

Of course, the Shap granite is just one small fraction of a large granite batholith that underlies the entire Lake District, and a recent model (Figure 2.21) suggests that the granite ridge changes in density from east to west. If you look carefully on Plate 1.1 you should be able to recognize the northerly extension of this ridge to the Skiddaw granite. But what happens along its southern boundary?

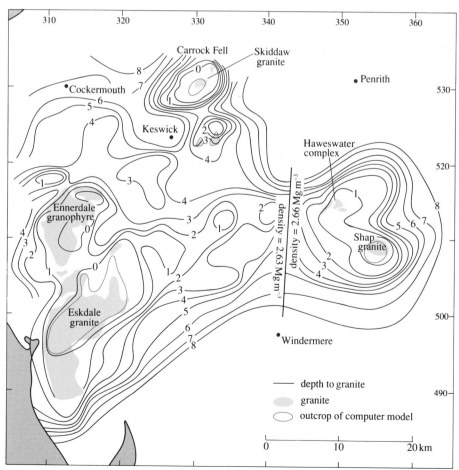

Figure 2.21 Contour map of the depth to the top of granite bodies across the Lake District batholith showing a base at $c.\ 9$ km.

Can you account for the steep dip of the Lake District batholith in the south?

This boundary corresponds almost exactly with the location of a buried magnetic, early Palaeozoic basement ridge (Plate 1.2) suggesting that the emplacement of the batholith could in some way have been controlled by this ridge.

Further to the southeast, and this time coincident with the basement ridge, are the gravity low of the Wensleydale granite (centred on GR390480—see also Figure 2.14) and flanking magnetic high. In contrast, the buried Weardale granite (centred on GR390540) has a stronger, sharper gravity anomaly but no magnetic signature, except perhaps a deficiency of magnetic sources, producing a weak magnetic low.

Gravity models by M. H. P. Bott and co-workers at Durham University of these two large buried granite masses in the North Pennines (Figures 2.22a and b) emphasize the relatively steep-sided form of the Weardale granite and the rather gentle dips on the flanks of the Wensleydale intrusion. Notice also how both intrusions have only a thin cover of Carboniferous; as you probably know they have both been proved at a few hundred metres depth by drilling. The magnetic anomaly at Wensleydale has been modelled as arising principally from a thick zone of moderate susceptibility metasediments uplifted by the granite during emplacement and concentrated over its southern flank (Figure 2.22c). As modelled, this source is not just due to contact metamorphism, but rather to a c. 3 km thick zone of magnetic basement rocks, probably Lower Palaeozoic metasediments of the Tornquist Ridge. The rising Weardale granite encountered no such materials and therefore has no corresponding magnetic anomaly.

It should be clear to you by now that granite intrusions are an important component of the shallow crust in the Southern Caledonides, at least as far south as the central Pennines. The granites were formed in association with subduction processes and

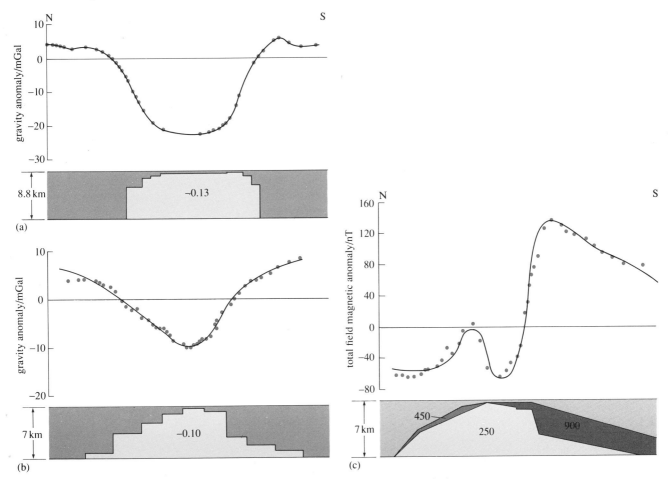

Figure 2.22 Modelled north–south cross-sections roughly along easting 390 through the Weardale (a) and Wensleydale (b, c) granite intrusions in the northern Pennines. (a) and (b) are gravity models with a density contrast given in 10^3 kg m^{-3}; (c) is a magnetic model. Red dots, observed values; black line, calculated curve. The susceptibilities shown are all × 10^6.

continental collision during closure of the Iapetus Ocean as described in Block 1A and in more detail in later Blocks. Further south, we have the postulated Market Weighton granite, the exposed Montsorrel intrusion (GR455315), and several other postulated buried intrusions, particularly around the Wash. In north Wales, there are also several small intrusions at outcrop level, but none of the distinctive anomalies that characterize the northern parts of the Southern Caledonides.

(d) *Variscan intrusions* The intense negative Bouguer gravity anomaly associated with the southwest England batholith is one of the most distinctive features of the gravity contour and relief map (Figure 2.11). Similar models exist to those described above, with the batholith extending to *c.* 20 km depth and all the outcropping intrusions lying on a buried granite ridge.

(e) *Tertiary intrusive complexes* As you will realize, having completed ITQ 2.5, we now switch to the most intense positive gravity anomalies in the UK. These are confined to the major Tertiary igneous centres of western Scotland, Northern Ireland (Figure 2.16) and the Bristol Channel. A little earlier, we stumbled across the paradoxical situation on Arran where a major positive gravity anomaly is associated with an outcropping low density granite.

> How common is this association? Examine the Ten Mile Map where the three strongest anomalies occur over Skye, Rhum and Mull.

The Skye intrusive centre includes granites in the east (the Red Hills) and both gabbros and ultrabasic rocks in the west (the Cuillin Hills). The Rhum centre contains the same rock types but with a good deal more ultrabasic material and less granite. The Mull centre contains roughly equal proportions of granite and gabbro with some ultrabasic rocks and some diorites.

> Does this provide any clues as to which rock types must be abundant at depth to account for the strong positive gravity (and magnetic) anomalies?

Basic, and particularly ultrabasic rocks have the appropriately high densities (3.03×10^3 and 3.15×10^3 kg m^{-3} average in Table 2.2) and high magnetic susceptibilities (6–13×10^{-3} average).

A gravity model (Figure 2.23) based on locally measured densities, which are therefore different from those in Table 2.2, shows that the granite body is just 2 km thick beneath the Red Hills, giving way downwards to a cylinder of high-density basic–ultrabasic rocks. This cylinder is easily interpreted as the conduit, or magma chamber, that fed the extensive Tertiary lava flows that occur over northwest Skye. It is exposed at the surface in the Cuillin Hills. (Note that although the model appears to show the cylinder extending only to 14 km depth, this is where the density contrast makes it difficult to resolve the basic and ultrabasic rocks from the dense lower/middle crust. The conduit rocks are therefore likely to extend below this depth).

Similar conclusions follow for all the other Tertiary igneous centres, including Lundy Island which, from potential field data, must also be sitting on top of a high-density column. The relative amounts of granite and basic–ultrabasic rocks exposed in these Tertiary centres depends on two factors: first, the extent of *partial melting* and *crystal fractionation* processes involved in making acid rocks (which we shall be examining in Blocks 2 and 3) and, second, the level of exposure—the centres are, of course, the *eroded remnants of central volcanoes associated with extensional tectonic processes*, such as are found in Iceland today. The main difference is that in the British Tertiary, the volumes of acid rocks are greater because of the availability of continental crust for melting in the incipient break-up of continents to form the North Atlantic. We shall be discussing these magmatic processes from a geochemical standpoint in Blocks 2 and 3.

Finally, there are some interesting magnetic anomaly contrasts across the Skye Igneous Centre, which you may have noticed when completing ITQ 2.5 (see Table A2). These are amplified in Figure 2.24, where we find a 250 nT positive anomaly over the Red Hills granites and a 250 nT negative anomaly over the Cuillin gabbros. Why does this occur when we appear, from the gravity data, to have a *single* basic–

ultrabasic cylinder? The most plausible interpretation is that a *reversal* of the Earth's magnetic field took place between the emplacement of the Cuillin gabbros and the Red Hills granites together with their associated high density substratum. So the magma conduit in Figure 2.23 must be made of two separate halves formed at different times, which are resolved by magnetic but not by gravity data. This is an excellent illustration of the combined use of different potential field methods to extract information on the structure and evolution of concealed geology.

2.3.3 Sedimentary basins

Like that of the central North Sea, the most obvious sedimentary basins associated with the British lithosphere are of Mesozoic–Tertiary age. You have already met some of these—apart from the North Sea, the more important ones are located in Figure 2.14.

> What is the common gravity and magnetic signature associated with Mesozoic–Tertiary sedimentary basins in the area around Britain?

Clearly, these sedimentary basins are responsible for most of the remaining dominant features on the Bouguer anomaly map. They all have negative gravity anomalies, but are generally characterized by smoothly varying, low magnitude negative magnetic anomalies. Gravity data tell us that the sedimentary rocks filling

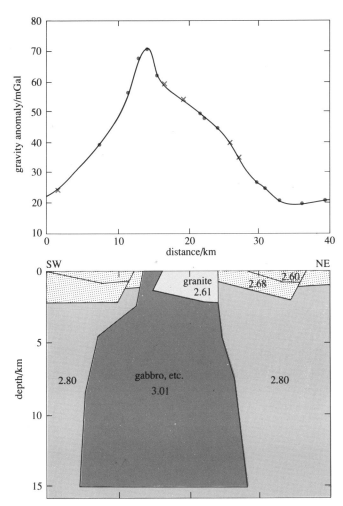

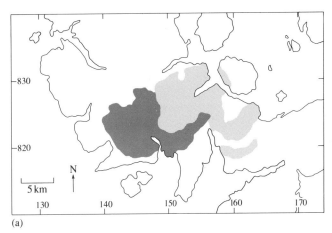

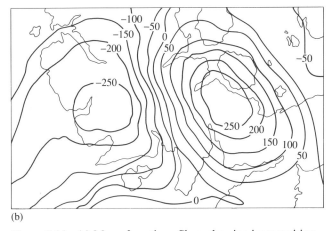

Figure 2.23 An interpretation of the subsurface structure of the Skye Tertiary Igneous Centre along a SW–NE line through the Red Hills granites and Cuillin gabbros. Crustal rocks are shown with stipple; the lower density is Jurassic and the higher Torridonian. Assumed densities of rock units are indicated in $10^3 \, \text{kg m}^{-3}$. Red dots on gravity curve represent values measured at gravity stations, red crosses represent values interpolated from a contour map and the black solid line is the computed gravity anomaly.

Figure 2.24 (a) Map of southern Skye, showing juxtaposition of intrusive centres at outcrop level in relation to national grid lines: grey shading, Cuillin gabbros; pink shading, Red Hills granite. (b) Total field magnetic anomaly map contoured at 50 nT intervals (see text for interpretation). (Note: the magnetic contributions from shallow sources, <5 km deep have been removed to show the effects of deeper sources.)

the basins must be of lower density than the surroundings, while magnetic data reflect the fact that magnetic sources are at considerable depth, buried beneath the pile of non-magnetic sedimentary rocks. Nevertheless, there are prominent positive magnetic anomalies, of 30–40 km width, beneath parts of the Moray Firth Basin, and these must reflect the continuation of the Great Glen Fault anomalies of mainland Scotland at greater depth to the northeast.

The shape of many of the basins is controlled by older, reactivated basement faults. For example, the northern margin of the Moray Firth Basin abuts the Helmsdale Fault; the southern margin of the Cheshire Basin abuts the Church Stretton Fault Zone, and the North Celtic Sea Basin is bounded by similar NE–SW structures of Caledonian trend. The Carboniferous (last movement) north–south Malvern Fault (see Section 2.3.1) provides the steep western boundary of the Worcester Basin, and there are likely to be similar deep fault controls on the shape of the Wessex and Yorkshire–Lincolnshire Basins.

As a simple example of basin structure, we shall look briefly at the early Mesozoic Cheshire Basin, which formed in a depression within the Carboniferous, itself controlled by a reactivated Caledonian Fault. The Bouguer anomaly minimum over the basin is -15 mGal (centred on GR380370) and since the regional field is about $+10$ mGal, the residual anomaly due to the basin must be about -25 mGal.

If the average density of the mainly Triassic sediments is 2.42×10^3 kg m^{-3} and that of the surrounding Carboniferous is 2.59×10^3 kg m^{-3}, what is the approximate thickness of the Cheshire Basin? ($G = 6.67 \times 10^{-11}$ N m^2 kg^{-2}.)

Equation 2.4 states $\Delta g = 2\pi G \ \Delta\rho \ t \times 10^5$ mGal, so $25 = 2\pi \times 6.67 \times 10^{-11} \times 0.17 \times 10^3 \times t \times 10^5$, whence $t = 3\,509$ m or about 3.5 km.

A computer model (Figure 2.25) shows that the basin extends to a maximum depth of 3.8 km, a little more than we have calculated because the basin is not 'infinite'. The average density we used probably does not compensate adequately for the low-density halites that are included in the model; their presence near the surface will have *reduced* the overall calculated thickness of the basin as shown in Figure 2.25. Notice also that, in this cross-section, the gravity gradient is steepest on the ESE side of the basin where the Church Stretton Fault Zone, through normal faulting, has downfaulted Carboniferous sediments to the west, providing a sharp basin margin.

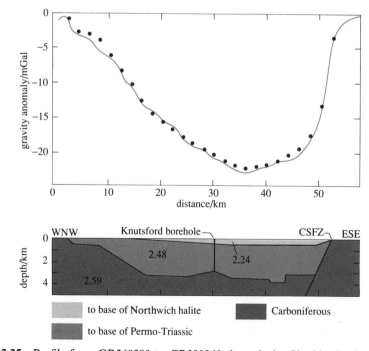

Figure 2.25 Profile from GR360380 to GR390360 through the Cheshire Basin showing observed residual gravity anomaly and the calculated effect of the model shown. CFSZ is the Church Stretton Fault Zone, as located in Figure 2.14. Red line, observed; black dots, calculated.

This example serves to illustrate the features of sedimentary basins that can be interpreted from potential field data. Of course, many other basins, some of smaller size, others of greater age, have been developed in and around Britain. For example, the Vale of Eden (GR360540), which we encountered in Section 2.3.1, is a small Permo-Triassic basin, and there are two, even smaller basins of this age around Dumfries in the Southern Uplands. You should locate these on the Ten Mile Map (GR300575 and 310585), and note their strong negative gravity anomalies in Plate 1.1, which are comparable in size with those of the Southern Uplands granite intrusions. Finally, we know that even older basins can be recognized, such as the Palaeozoic depression across Cardigan Bay (discussed in Section 2.2.2); this has a less prominent gravity signature, however, because the sedimentary fill has become more compact, lithified, and therefore more dense.

Summary

1   Section 2.3 has been concerned entirely with interpreting the gravity and magnetic anomaly patterns across the British lithosphere using colour contour maps, a shaded relief image (Figure 2.11) and combined contour–relief images of the Southern Uplands–northern England region (Plates 1.1 and 1.2). These have been used (a) to build up a general picture of the three-dimensional structure and associated trends that characterize the major tectonic zones and terranes of the UK, (b) to examine the deep geological features of known igneous intrusions, and complexes, to suggest the locations of concealed intrusions, and (c) to discuss briefly the location and structure of young sedimentary basins.

2   The east–west increase in gravity across Britain has been related to a combination of (a) the transition from low-density continental to higher-density oceanic lithosphere, (b) flexural uplift of western Britain in response to loading and subsidence of the North Sea basin, and (c) in the north, the transition from low-density Moine and Dalradian metasediments west towards uplifted high-density gneisses of the Hebridean craton. There is no *simple* corresponding magnetic effect, though the location of Tertiary oceanic extensional processes in northwestern Britain is reflected in the major magnetic anomalies over lava fields (shallow sources only) and intrusive complexes (shallow and deep sources).

3   On the Scottish mainland, strong potential field gradients follow a NE–SW trend along the major Caledonian faults. A line of deeply buried (intrusive?) magnetic sources over the Great Glen Fault extends northeast under the Moray Firth Basin gravity low. Otherwise, north of the Highland Boundary Fault, the whole of Scotland looks like a single terrane punctured by Caledonian intrusions. These include early orogenic 'granites' that are small in volume and have higher densities than large volume late granites, some of which extend to 13 km depth (Figure 2.17). Some of these late granites also have magnetic aureoles and root zones, probably resulting from thermal dehydrative metamorphism of pre-existing metasediments, producing magnetite. But the strongest magnetic anomalies in Caledonian northern Scotland occur over the Aberdeenshire Gabbros, which, geophysically, are dense magnetic slabs, some 5–10 km wide and thick.

4   The Midland Valley is a distinctive region of elevated Bouguer gravity, suggesting that the low-density Upper Palaeozoic sedimentary cover is a thin capping (a few kilometres thick) overlying high-density basement. Variable magnetic anomalies reflect a combination of exposed Carboniferous basic lavas (magnetic rough zones) and vents (smooth magnetic highs) with deep root zones that can also be traced as gravity highs (e.g. at Stonehaven and Bathgate, Figure 2.18). A concealed Caledonian granite is postulated beneath the Hamilton area.

5   Extending from the North Sea across to Northern Ireland along the Southern Uplands Fault is a thin line of magnetic highs, probably associated with ophiolites at the base of the Southern Uplands accretionary prism (as exposed at Ballantrae). Gravity is lower across the Southern Uplands and further south than in the Midland Valley, reflecting the greater thickness of Lower Palaeozoic low-grade metasediments south of the Southern Uplands Fault. The NE–SW broad magnetic high across the central Southern Uplands may result from a subducted ocean lithosphere

source beneath the crust, perhaps the ultimate source of magmas that rose to form steep-sided intrusive granites (see gravity anomalies in Plate 1.1 and models in Figures 2.9 and 2.19).

6   An important influence over potential field anomalies across the Southern Caledonides is the presence of the Midlands Craton, of Cadomian (late Precambrian) age, which is not well exposed at the surface. The eastern part, an extension of the NW–SE trending London–Brabant massif, seems to abut the western part, which has normal NE–SW Caledonian trends, along the north–south Malvern Fault (Figure 2.14). Further basement ridges, partly Cadomian, partly Caledonian (especially further north) are wrapped around the Midlands Craton. An easterly segment passes beneath East Anglia, Lincolnshire, and Yorkshire, and joins, in south Cumbria, a westerly segment that underlies the Irish Sea. Cadomian-aged basement also occurs along the basement high through Anglesey, but this appears to be separated from the main craton by the Welsh Basin (Block 1A, Figure 3.23).

This arcuate pattern of potential field anomalies is one of the most distinctive differences between the Northern and Southern Caledonides. It is thought to reflect processes during the closure of the NE–SW aligned Iapetus Ocean and the NW–SE oriented Tornquist Sea (Figure 2.13) when the Midlands Craton moved north towards an embayment in the northern shoreline of the Caledonian ocean. At this stage, Lower Palaeozoic volcaniclastic rocks would have been compressed to form prominent ridges, now buried around the margins of the craton.

7   Emplaced within and to the north of these arcuate basement ridges in the Southern Caledonides is a major line of late Caledonian (c. 400 Ma old) granite intrusions, including concealed batholiths beneath Wensleydale and Weardale in the north Pennines, and a largely concealed batholith beneath the central Lake District (Figures 2.20 to 2.22). Again, magnetic anomalies occur in association with granite intrusions, partricularly where suitable iron-rich country rocks exist in the aureole for magnetite to be produced during thermal metamorphism. The magnetic anomaly over Wensleydale, however, probably results from the uplift of a 3–4 km thick zone of moderately magnetic metasediments of the Tornquist ridge (Plate 1.2). Isolated smaller granitic intrusions occur further south in the English–Welsh Caledonian terrane, and some have been located beneath Mesozoic cover using potential field methods.

8   There is some potential field evidence for the location of the Variscan Front, and for the thin-skinned nature of the Devonian and Carboniferous sediments that were carried north across southern Britain over variable topography on low-angle thrusts (Figure 2.15). But the main features revealed by the potential field maps in this area have developed since Variscan thrusting occurred, and include: (a) the broad, deep Mesozoic Wessex Basin centred beneath Hampshire but extending east towards southeast England; (b) the 200 km eastwards continuation of the anomalies over the Lizard ophiolite, probaby marking the line where another Variscan thrust reaches the surface; (c) the large volume, 10–20 km deep, granite batholith beneath southwest England; and (d) the magnetic anomalies due to reversed NRM sources, possibly Devonian basalts, along the northern batholith margin.

9   The Tertiary intrusive centres (Figure 2.16) along the west coast of Britain (see 2 above) gave rise to extensive lava fields and dyke swarms that are easily traced magnetically (see, for example, Plate 1.2). At the surface, within the centres themselves, we find mixtures of granite, gabbro and ultrabasic rocks. Gravity and magnetic data confirm that basic–ultrabasic material is much the more important at depth (Figure 2.23) occurring in 'cylindrical' magma feeder pipes that tapped mantle magma source regions during extensional volcanism.

10   Mesozoic sedimentary basins in and around Britain are located by means of their strong negative gravity anomalies and generally subdued magnetic signature. Positive gravity anomalies may occur over major grabens such as the central North Sea because of lithospheric thinning and magma emplacement. Basin shapes are often dictated by the presence of old basement faults, which become reactivated and may affect the Upper Palaeozoic foundations on which many of these basins are built.

SAQS FOR SECTION 2

SAQ 2.1 In two or three sentences each, explain what is meant by the following terms and the way in which they are used to isolate or interpret lithospheric potential field anomalies:

      (a)   IGF   (b)   IGRF

      (c)   NRM   (d)   Regional fields

SAQ 2.2 State, with reasons, whether each of the following statements is true or false:

(a) The flattening of the Earth means that more mass is concentrated around the equator, making values of gravitational acceleration larger there than over the poles.

(b) Given that the Cairnsmore of Fleet granite (GR260570) has a $-24\,\text{mGal}$ residual anomaly and a density contrast compared with its surroundings of $-140\,\text{kg m}^{-3}$, it cannot be more than 4 km thick.

(c) The steepest marginal gravity gradients around Mesozoic sedimentary basins developed in and around Britain are associated with deep faults beneath the associated basin margin.

(d) The small magnetic low just north of the annular positive magnetic anomaly around the Cheviot granite (GR390620) indicates that the source has a strong NRM due to crystallization in a field opposite to that of the present-day Earth.

(e) The gravity lows over northern Scotland (north of the Highland Boundary Fault) are due to a combination of thick low density Moine and Dalradian metasediments and low density 'late' Caledonian granite intrusions.

(f) The different magnetic anomaly patterns over the Weardale and Wensleydale granites are thought to result from the intrusion of the latter into a magnetized Tornquist basement ridge; the Weardale intrusion encountered no such materials.

SAQ 2.3 With reference to the Midlands Craton, describe briefly:

(a) the potential field evidence for the existence of the craton beneath an area of Upper Palaeozoic-Mesozoic cover; and

(b) the criteria that have been used to define (approximately) its northern boundary.

SAQ 2.4 In a sentence each, what is the evidence for the following assertions:

(a) The British Tertiary lavas were crystallized during a period of reversed geomagnetic polarity.

(b) The SW England batholith continues at least 100 km beyond the tip of Cornwall (Land's End).

(c) The strong, narrow magnetic anomaly centred over the Shap granite (GR360510) is not due simply to the granite itself.

(d) The Strath Halladale granite (see Figure 2.14) is either of low volume or of average crustal density for this part of the Highlands.

3 SEISMOLOGICAL STUDIES

Although we have come a long way in our understanding of the broad structure of the British lithosphere using potential field techniques, including the identification of separate basement terranes and the recognition and approximate geometry of intrusive complexes and sedimentary basins, many questions remain unanswered. For example, we have no information on the deep layering of the crust and upper mantle beneath Britain, and have been unable to define the sub-surface geometry of major thrusts and fault zones (e.g. the Moine Thrust, the Iapetus Suture and the Variscan Front). Seismic techniques offer the potential for amplifying our knowledge of the lithosphere because they involve the passage of *elastic waves* through the Earth, and the analysis of the arrival times for these waves at detectors to deduce the *velocity structure*—the geometry of boundaries between different geological units and the seismic wave speeds within each unit. In general, active

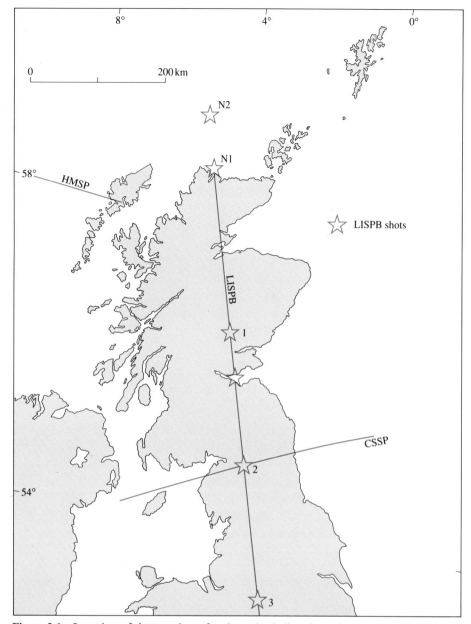

Figure 3.1 Location of three major refraction seismic lines in and around mainland UK: LISPB—Lithospheric Seismic Profile in Britain; CSSP—Caledonian Suture Seismic Project; HMSP—Hebridean Margin Seismic Project.

techniques are more useful than earthquake seismology because of the greater control over source—detector geometry available with man-made explosions. In the last 10–15 years, enormous strides have been made in seismic data acquisition and processing technologies for deep lithosphere seismic studies as well as for the more obvious applications in hydrocarbon exploration. Although many of the advances have focused on *reflection* seismology, which has been applied extensively during the 1980s to off-shore areas around the coast of Britain (Section 3.2) we start with three *refraction* lines run in and around mainland UK since 1974 (Figure 3.1). Both the reflection and refraction measurements that we shall discuss were obtained using man-made explosions, usually at sea, but the main north–south refraction line shown in Figure 3.1 also included some large on-land explosions detonated in deep boreholes drilled for the purpose.

As in Section 2, we shall comment briefly on the principles and applications of each technique, and then concentrate mainly on the results that have been obtained and their geological/tectonic interpretation. One further point, in what follows we have used the term *velocity* rather than *speed* when describing the propagation of seismic waves in rocks. This follows the common recognition in geophysics that seismic waves are defined by the way they propagate and are measured, hence the use of the vector term velocity which, strictly, has magnitude and direction whereas speed is scalar and has only magnitude.

3.1 REFRACTION SEISMOLOGY

The basis of this technique should be fairly familiar to you from earlier courses. It involves waves travelling from source to detectors being refracted, or bent at boundaries where there is a change in propagation velocity. We aim to locate these boundaries and the velocities of waves between them. To appreciate how this is done we shall examine the simplest case of horizontal layers.

3.1.1 Basic principles

Seismic waves travel out into the Earth from a source in all directions: these are known as body waves, as opposed to surface waves that are restricted to the vicinity of the Earth's surface. In the case of two layers with a horizontal boundary and a downwards increase in velocity (Figure 3.2), we are concerned with only two paths away from S: along the surface towards D and downwards towards A.

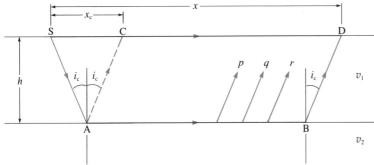

Figure 3.2 The travel paths of elastic waves (red) from a seismic source S situated at the surface of a two-layer system. The velocities of the waves in the upper and lower layers are v_1 and v_2, respectively, where $v_2 > v_1$. The angle of incidence in this diagram is equal to the critical angle, so the refracted wave travels along the path AB in the lower layer. Secondary waves emitted along AB (such as p, q, r) are refracted back into the upper layer and may be detected at the surface.

What do we call the wave that travels along the surface from S to D?

This is known as the *direct wave*; it takes the shortest path from source to detector. (Note that it is a body wave travelling parallel to the surface.)

The particular angle which the wave following SA makes with the vertical at A, known as the *critical angle of incidence* (i_c), is defined by the ratio of wave velocities in the two layers, such that

$$\sin i_c = \frac{v_1}{v_2} \tag{3.1}$$

Why are we interested in this particular wave path rather than ones that strike the boundary at a greater or lesser angle than i_c?

The wave must arrive at exactly the critical angle in order to refract and propagate *along* the interlayer boundary, but within the lower layer, where it can act as a source of secondary waves propagating back to the surface. If the wave struck the boundary at a greater angle it would be reflected without passing into the lower layer; if it struck at a smaller angle it would be refracted (away from the normal to the boundary AB) into the lower layer but would not run along the boundary.

Waves that have penetrated the second layer and have followed paths such as SABD back to the surface are known as *refracted waves*. Those along p, q, r and other paths parallel to this direction would all be detected if there was a line of detectors between S and D, but it is clear from the diagram that there is no refracted wave between S and C, known as the *critical distance* (x_c, which is defined geometrically as $2h \tan i_c$). Beyond C, there will be two arrivals, the direct wave and the refracted wave, but which arrives first depends on the distance (x), the two velocities v_1 and v_2, and

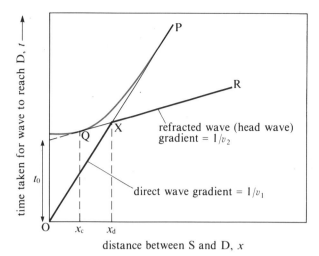

Figure 3.3 The time–distance graph for the situation shown in Figure 3.2. OP represents the direct wave arriving at D, and QR represents the refracted wave. The first wave to arrive at D is represented by the heavy line OXR. For $x < x_d$, this is the direct wave; but at $x > x_d$, the refracted wave becomes the first arrival. No refracted wave arrives at all at D when $x < x_c$. The red line is the time–distance curve for waves reflected at the boundary between the upper and lower layers.

the thickness (h) of the upper layer. However, it should be clear that with increasing values of x, a point is reached at which refracted waves that have spent a significant part of their history in the deeper, higher velocity layer will reach a detector *before* the direct wave. This point, at which the refracted wave overtakes the direct wave, is called the **cross-over distance** (x_d) and is illustrated in Figure 3.3, where the travel time (t) of the first seismic wave arrival at each detector is plotted against the distance from S to that detector. The line OP represents the variation in arrival time for the direct wave with increasing distance, so the inverse of the gradient gives the upper layer velocity (v_1). QR represents refracted wave arrivals and, similarly, has a gradient $1/v_2$. A back-projection of this line to the time axis gives the intercept t_0. The thickness of the upper layer can then be calculated from these parameters as:

$$h = \frac{x_d}{2}\sqrt{\frac{v_2 - v_1}{v_2 + v_1}}, \text{ or } h = \frac{t_0\, v_1\, v_2}{2\sqrt{v_2{}^2 - v_1{}^2}} \tag{3.2}$$

ITQ 3.1 Assuming that the surface of the Earth approximates to the horizontal over short distances, at what distance from a source would refracted waves from the continental Moho become the first arrivals at detectors? (Typical crust and mantle seismic wave velocities are 6.5 and 8.0 km s^{-1}, and a typical Moho depth is 35 km.)

The results of this calculation should enable you to understand why the three long seismic refraction lines in Figure 3.1 have lengths of several hundred kilometres. Without introducing further complications, it should be clear, intuitively, that we would increase the complexity of Figures 3.2 and 3.3, including the mathematics involved, to obtain solutions for multiple layer problems in which some of the layers are dipping. In general, the more data that are available, the more unique a geological model can be calculated. This is done using **ray tracing** techniques, whereby the paths of seismic waves (i.e. the 'rays' represented in Figure 3.2) are continuously adjusted by fitting models with different boundary thicknesses and slopes until the best match is obtained with the observed travel time data. Modern seismology also involves matching the amplitudes of seismic disturbances as well as the travel times.

As you may know from studying the physical properties of light, strictly, waves propagate as a series of moving **wave fronts** (Figure 3.4), but a convenient way of describing **wave paths** is to use 'rays' drawn at right angles to the wave front. Seismic wave propagation can be described in the same way, and in the next part of the video sequence you will see Figure 3.4 being constructed by David Smythe of Glasgow University. He also discusses the results of the **LISPB** (the **Lithospheric Seismic**

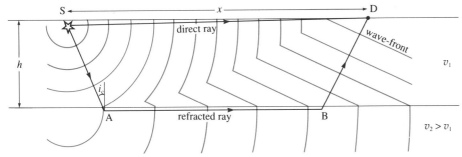

Figure 3.4 Two-dimensional representation of the successive positions (at equal time intervals) of expanding spherical wave fronts (red) from a seismic source (S) in a two-layer case identical to Figure 3.2. Rays or wave paths, can be drawn at right angles to the wave front at any location. In the upper layer, the wave front represents the *first* disturbance to arrive at any location, so the upward migrating refracted waves can be seen gradually overtaking near-surface disturbances, which have stayed entirely in the upper layer, beneath S to D. (Strictly, the terms 'wave path' and 'ray' are synonymous.)

Profile in Britain) refraction experiment—the 600 km long north–south line in Figure 3.1 from the north of Scotland to the south Pennines. You should now view the next seven minutes of the video programme: *Fragments of Britain* on videocassette VC 271 starting after the Hipkin gravity sequence (13 minutes on the clock) and stopping after the results of the LISPB experiment have been summarized (20 minutes on the clock).

We shall look at the LISPB results again in a moment, but first we need one more piece of theory. It is often the case in large-scale refraction studies of the deep lithosphere that subtle changes in velocity are sought which are difficult to distinguish on conventional time–distance graphs (Figure 3.3). **Reduced time–distance graphs** are then employed in which, instead of plotting time (t) against distance (x), the quantity plotted against distance is:

$$t - \frac{x}{v_0} \tag{3.3}$$

where v_0 is usually chosen to be a typical upper layer velocity, often 6 km s^{-1}. On such graphs (e.g. Figure 3.5) the sequence of time–distance lines is exactly as before, but the gradients of the lines are:

$$\text{gradient} = \frac{1}{v} - \frac{1}{v_0} \text{ s km}^{-1} \tag{3.4}$$

where v is the velocity in any layer being considered and v_0 is the chosen reference velocity.

> What, then, will be the gradient of the reduced time–distance line for a layer in which the velocity is identical to the reference velocity, v_0?

The gradient will be zero, so the line will be horizontal.

Layers with velocities greater than v_0 will produce *negative* gradients (because $1/v$ is then smaller than $1/v_0$ in equation 3.4), and layers with velocities less than v_0 will produce positive gradients. The equations for determining the thickness of the upper layer can be applied as before.

> **ITQ 3.2** To increase your familiarity with reduced time–distance graphs, calculate the velocity and thickness of the upper layer and the velocity of the lower layer in Figure 3.5. (Note that $v_0 = 6.0$ km s^{-1} has been used.)

If you think these calculations are a bit tedious, we sympathize, but you will soon appreciate the value of reduced time–distance graphs, which is that they provide an immediate visual impression of the departures from a chosen reference velocity, v_0.

A final point about seismic refraction surveys is that they are most easily interpreted in areas where there is relatively little geological complexity because refraction models become blurred by changes in layer thickness, velocity or dip. A primary requirement is that velocity increases with depth so that wave paths (rays) are bent away from the normal to an interface (Figure 3.2), producing critical angle

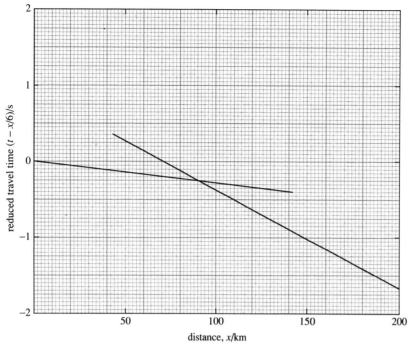

Figure 3.5 Reduced travel time–distance graph for use with ITQ 3.2.

refractions. If velocity *decreases* downwards the wave path is bent *towards* the normal, and this straightening means there will be no critical refractions into the low-velocity layer, and thus no refracted wave at the surface. Not only are low-velocity layers difficult to identify in seismic refraction surveys, but their presence leads to erroneous calculated depths to lower layers. Of course, seismic refraction surveys are cheaper and easier to process than reflection surveys, but, as you will see, the information they yield is much more limited. Nevertheless, they do have the advantage over reflection methods of yielding velocities directly from travel time graphs.

3.1.2 Seismic refraction profiles of Britain

The three experiments of particular interest to us are (cf. Figure 3.1) LISPB, **CSSP (Caledonian Suture Seismic Project)** and **HMSP (Hebridean Margin Seismic Project)**. The LISPB experiment was carried out in 1974 with the stated aims of:

(a)   establishing a reliable seismic velocity cross-section of the lithosphere through the British Isles;

(b)   contributing to the discussions of tectonic problems in the British Isles, particularly the evolution of the Caledonides; and

(c)   providing a basis, through enhanced knowledge of deep seismic velocities, for future long-range profiles designed to investigate the lower (sub-crustal) lithosphere.

The CSSP in 1982 had a similar target, to determine the lithospheric velocity structure south of the Iapetus Suture; the HMSP of 1975 was somewhat different, aiming to investigate the structure of the continental–oceanic transition west of the Hebrides.

LISPB

Shots were fired at the six shot-points marked on Figure 3.1 and were received at 5–10 km intervals along the profile to obtain a series of overlapping and reversed profiles. An example of the data obtained is shown in Figure 3.6, where seismograms are plotted at the relevant distance from the northernmost shot point (N2). We have marked first arrival reduced time–distance lines for you as a_1 and d.

> **ITQ 3.3**   What are the velocities defined by the lines a_1 and d, and which lithospheric layers might these arrivals come from? (For d, use arrivals between 190 and 230 km along the profile, and again use $v_0 = 6$ km s^{-1}. Remember that seismic velocity data for different rock types are given in Table 2.2.)

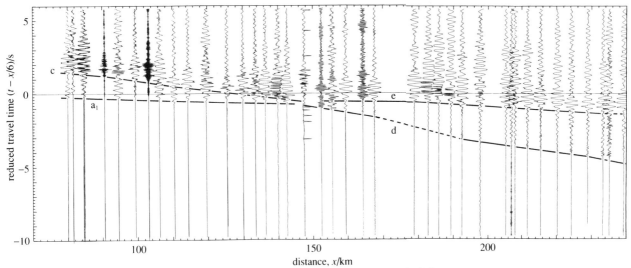

Figure 3.6 Reduced travel time ($t - x/6$ seconds) plotted against distance (x, km) for a section of LISPB showing recorded seismograms and the arrival 'phases' (i.e. signals forming a coherent set of arrivals) a_1, c, d and e. Distances are given in kilometres south of the northernmost shot point (N2 in Figure 3.1).

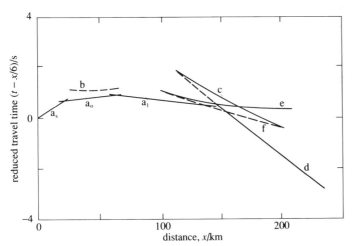

Figure 3.7 Summary of LISPB reduced travel time–distance curves; reduced travel time ($t - x/6$ seconds) plotted against distance (x, km). Solid lines indicate arrivals seen on several sections; broken lines represent those seen on only a few sections. The labels indicate the arrival phases, which represent refractions (a, f, d) and reflections (b, c, e) from different layers as summarized in Figure 3.8 and Table 3.1.

Some strong signals marked c and e on Figure 3.6 are, in fact, reflected wave arrivals, respectively, from the Moho and from a boundary within the lower crust. Signals such as these were helpful in constraining the overall analysis of LISPB data but need concern us no further here. A summary of all the signals identified on LISPB is given in Figure 3.7. Close to the shot-point, in some sections of the profile we have a_s arrivals, which represent the direct wave through the uppermost layers with a velocity of c. 4–5 km s^{-1}; almost everywhere an a_0 set of arrivals was found, representing refractions from the main upper crustal layer with a velocity in the range 5.5–6.2 km s^{-1} (in Figure 3.7, a_0 has a velocity just less than 6 km s^{-1}). The arrivals marked b are another reflection, this time from the mid-crust, and f is a lower crustal refraction from the same depth as the e reflections. In summary, in addition to a sedimentary a_s layer that occurs in some areas, LISPB identified a three-layer crust beneath northern Britain, giving rise to time–distance refracted arrival lines a_0, a_1 and f, with Moho refractions (due to 8 km s^{-1} mantle) forming the d line. Notice also the short cross-over distance to mantle arrivals at around 150 km (Figures 3.6 and 3.7) implying that the Moho is rather shallow in comparison with the typical depth of 35 km we assumed in ITQ 3.1 (where x_d was 218 km).

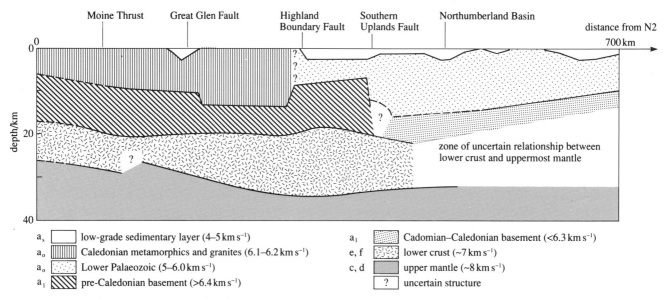

Figure 3.8 Velocity–depth cartoon and preliminary geological interpretation for the crust and uppermost mantle of northern Britain as deduced from the LISPB seismic refraction experiment. Note that many of the interfaces shown, rather than being sharp, are more likely to be zones across which velocity changes gradually.

Table 3.1 Lithospheric layering interpreted from the LISPB profile of Britain

Layer	Associated signals on seismograms	North of the Highland Boundary Fault				South of the Southern Uplands Fault			
		Depth to top/km	Depth to bottom/km	Velocity km s^{-1}	Rock type	Depth to top/km	Depth to bottom/km	Velocity km s^{-1}	Rock type
Superficial	a_s	0	0–4	4.0–5.0	sedimentary	0	0–5	4.0–5.0	sedimentary
Upper crust	a_0	0–4	6–14	6.1–6.2	Moine-Dalradian and granites	0–5	8–15	5.6–6.0	Lower Palaeozoic metasediments and granites
Middle crust*	a_1	6–14	$c.$ 20	6.48	granulite basement (Lewisian in North)	8–15	12–22	6.28	Cadomian–Caledonian basement
Lower crust	e, f	$c.$ 20	25–35	7.0	unknown	?	?	?	?
Upper mantle	c, d	25–35	—	8.0	peridotite	?	—	8.0	peridotite

*The a_1 layer is often taken together with the a_0 layer as part of a two-layer upper crust in Britain.

The reduced time–distance graphs for the entire profile were interpreted to give the velocity–depth cartoon shown in Figure 3.8 and in the video programme, and the details together with some geological interpretation are given in Table 3.1. At this point, we should emphasize that the three-layered crustal structure is partly an artefact of the modelling techniques used in the original interpretation of LISPB. Recent remodelling suggests that the sharp interfaces shown in Figure 3.8 are each better interpreted as zones of rapid velocity change with depth, perhaps due to a series of small discontinuities. Nevertheless, Figure 3.8 shows quite clearly that a major change in the velocity structure of the crust occurs across the Midland Valley and, in particular, at the Southern Uplands Fault. The following contrasts are important:

(a)   the upper crustal a_0 metasedimentary layer thins dramatically and reduces velocity from north to south across the Highland Boundary Fault, the latter presumably reflecting the change from high to low metamorphic grades across the fault;

(b)   the Lower Palaeozoic a_0 layer thickens dramatically from $c.\,5$ km to 15 km across the Southern Uplands Fault and remains about 10 km thick at the south end of the section;

(c)   the mid-crustal (or lowermost upper crust—see Table 3.1 footnote) 'granulite' a_1 layer steps up across the Midland Valley and continues south to the Southern Uplands Fault, where it is replaced by a thinner, deeper Cadomian–Caledonian basement layer with slightly lower seismic velocity;

(d)   a high-velocity lower crustal f layer of unknown composition occurs beneath northern Scotland with a well-defined Moho at its base, and runs south to the Southern Uplands area, where it is replaced to the south by a zone of uncertain crust–mantle relationships.

How consistent are observations (a)–(c) with our earlier deductions from potential field data about the deep structure of the Midland Valley relative to the adjacent areas?

The LISPB profile amplifies and supports our earlier conclusion that high density basement occurs at shallower depth beneath the Midland Valley. However, it is perhaps surprising that the medium-grade metasedimentary a_0 layer has a slightly higher velocity north of the Highland Boundary, where gravity is much lower than over the same thickness of lower-velocity Lower Palaeozoics south of the Southern Uplands Fault. The reasons are not fully understood, but are probably connected with the occurrence of more upper crustal granites in northern Scotland, giving a lower density but a higher seismic velocity than further south. Nevertheless, low-density granites usually have velocities less than 6 km s^{-1}, and the higher grades of metamorphism in the north must also be a significant factor in determining the a_0 layer velocities of 6.1–6.2 km s^{-1}.

Although the LISPB seismic refraction profile, like the potential field data, identifies three separate terranes—the Northern Caledonides and the Southern Caledonides with the Midland Valley between—it was unable to identify the Iapetus Suture itself, probably because refraction methods are not well suited to resolving dipping structures. Moreover, the displacements on the Moine Thrust (at the extreme north of the section between shot-points N1 and N2) and Great Glen Fault were not recognized; no significant offsetting of the different crustal layers was detected.

So, considering its initial aims, was the LISPB experiment a success? Well, at least it was partly successful in providing a general model of the crustal layering in Britain, which has since been invaluable in the analysis of later seismic investigations. The experiment showed that a major change in velocity structure occurs in the vicinity of the Midland Valley of Scotland, but it failed to provide much data relating to the Iapetus Suture, the deep structure in the south, or some of the more vertical structures, for which, of course, the method is also not well suited.

CSSP

The aim of this project was to clarify some of the uncertain results of LISPB by undertaking a seismic experiment in the Southern Caledonides but almost at right angles to LISPB, parallel to and just south of the supposed site of the Iapetus Suture. Shots were detonated in the North Sea and Irish Sea at either end of the line and detected by a series of on-land receivers following a WNW–ESE line through Carlisle. To a large extent, CSSP was a success; in the terminology of Figures 3.6 and 3.7, c-type, d-type and e-type arrivals were obtained (Figure 3.9)—so the Moho was defined—together with three sets of a-type arrivals. One of these, due to arrivals from the third layer down, the a_1 layer, was the first arrival at shot-detector distances ranging from just 30 km to about 130 km—it is the only a-type arrival shown in Figure 3.9.

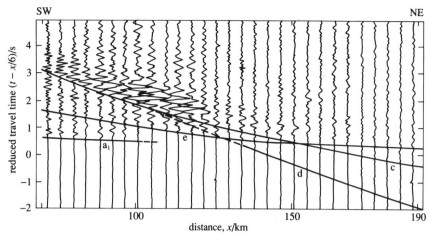

Figure 3.9 Reduced travel time ($t - x/6$ seconds) against distance (x, km) plot from the CSSP experiment, showing the arrivals of refracted waves (a_1, d) and reflected waves (c, e), using the same nomenclature as given on the LISPB diagrams. (Arrivals are recorded at a single receiver in northern England (15 km NNE of LISPB shot-point 2 on Figure 3.1). Distances are given in kilometres from a series of North Sea shot-points located along the CSSP line (Figure 3.1) between 10 and 130 km off the Northumberland Coast.)

What does this imply about the thickness of the two shallower layers (a_s and a_0) as compared with northern Scotland?

The uppermost layers must be *thin*—or have very low seismic velocities—in comparison with their *c.* 10 km thickness further north (Figure 3.8), where the a_0–a_1 cross-over distance is *c.* 60 km.

A picture of the upper crustal velocity structure and geological interpretation (Figure 3.10) identifies the shallowest (a_s) layer as Carboniferous across the Pennine axis, and the next (a_0) layer as Lower Palaeozoic metasedimentary rocks. The line of section crosses to the north of the Weardale pluton gravity low (Plate 1.1), thus avoiding the complications of shallow intrusive bodies. The combined thickness of these two upper layers is *c.* 4 km and they overlie the *c.* 13 km thick, ubiquitous a_1 layer, which has a velocity of 6.15 km s^{-1}.

ITQ 3.4   A summary of all the layers and boundaries identified by CSSP is given in Table 3.2. What are the differences between this and the velocity structure deduced by the LISPB experiment across the appropriate part of the Southern Caledonides (i.e. around the Northumberland Basin)?

If the comparison between LISPB and CSSP seems complicated, remember two things: (i) that the combined thickness of the upper crustal layers (17–20 km) is

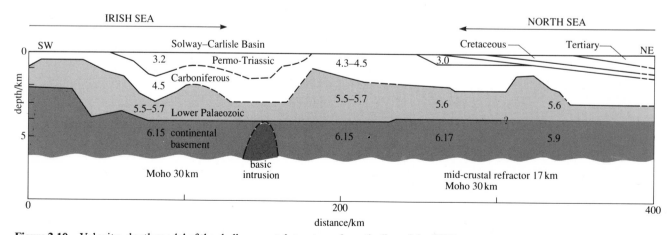

Figure 3.10   Velocity–depth model of the shallow crustal structure along the line of the CSSP experiment. Velocities are in km s^{-1}. The differences between this structure and that of LISPB in the same area are the subject of ITQ 3.4. The basic intrusion beneath the Carlisle Basin is inferred from aeromagnetic data (anomaly at GR330560 on the aeromagnetic map).

Table 3.2 Lithospheric layering interpreted from the CSSP profile of northern England

Layer	Depth to top/km	Depth to bottom/km	Velocity/km s^{-1}	Rock type
Upper crust I	0	0.5–3	3.2–4.5	Permo-Triassic and Carboniferous sediments
	0.5–3	2–4	5.5–5.7	Lower Palaeozoic metasediments
Upper crust II	2–4	c. 17	6.15	Pre-Caledonian basement?
Lower crust	c. 17	30	6.6	?
Upper mantle	30	—	8.0	peridotite

almost identical where the profiles cross, and (ii) that the total crustal thickness on CSSP is what we might expect from the LISPB data further north. The definition and resolution of seismic layers in northern England is much better on CSSP than LISPB, so the obvious question we must ask is—what geological explanation satisfies the seismic constraints for the important 6.15 km s^{-1} layer?

According to the original interpretation of the CSSP data, this major upper crustal layer was designated as 'pre-Caledonian basement'. The reasoning is as follows: 6.15 km s^{-1} is too slow a velocity for ocean crust so it cannot be the elusive Iapetus oceanic lithosphere that we hope to find buried in this region. Another possibility is that the 5.6–6.15 km s^{-1} layer boundary represents a metamorphic transition to a higher grade facies within the lower Palaeozoic sequence. The argument against this is that the boundary is not gradational enough, but appears to be too sharp for a metamorphic transition. This leaves older basement as the third possibility.

What do you think might be the objection to this interpretation?

If pre-Caledonian basement is present at depths less than 5 km, it seems surprising that there is no evidence for its presence either at outcrop or on the potential field images (Plates 1.1 and 1.2).

In our examination of the latter, we concluded that Lower Palaeozoic volcaniclastics wrapped around the Midlands Craton occupy much of the crustal volume in northern England. Thus the geological interpretation of the major upper crustal layer on CSSP remains uncertain, and further comments on this area must await our synthesis of seismic reflection data in the Caledonian Suture Zone (Section 3.2). Despite this debate over the interpretation of the a$_1$ layer velocity, CSSP was successful in providing information on lithospheric structure south of the Iapetus Suture.

HMSP

Earlier, in Section 2.3.1, we examined the increase in regional gravity across the western margin of the European continent. The HMSP project, where a line of large shots were fired at sea out to 300 km due west of Lewis, with arrivals being recorded at detectors on the Scottish mainland, offers the opportunity to study this ocean–continent transition. The main objective was to determine whether the transition is gradational or abrupt.

The data were interpreted as a simple three-layer model (Figure 3.11) of sedimentary cover, basement of the Hebridean Craton and upper mantle. At the eastern end, the Moho occurs at 27 km depth, in good agreement with LISPB (Figure 3.8), and the crust thins gradually across c. 100 km along the seismic line to reach 18 km thickness at the western end of the line.

Is this a reasonable thickness for oceanic crust?

No, oceanic crust is normally about 8 km thick. So, we would need to look even further west to find true oceanic crust, perhaps crossing another step like the one shown in Figure 3.11. This gradation from continental to oceanic lithosphere

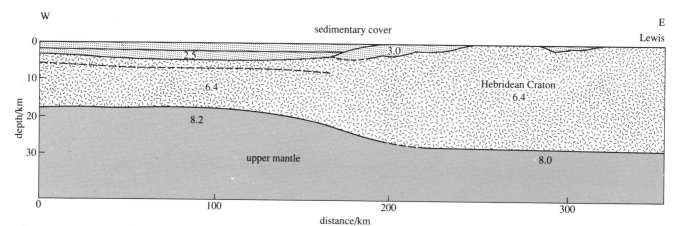

Figure 3.11 Velocity–depth model of the crustal structure across the Hebridean oceanic–continental margin as deduced from the HMSP experiment. Velocities are given in km s^{-1}, and the profile runs 300 km due west of the Isle of Lewis (Figure 3.1).

characterizes many past extensional continental margins that have undergone a complex history of faulting and thinning during extension. Nevertheless, the shallower mantle at the western end of the HMSP seismic line is quite enough to account for increased Bouguer gravity in this region (see extreme northwest corner of the Bouguer anomaly map). If the 9 km crustal thinning replaces lower crustal rocks of density 2.9×10^3 kg m^{-3} with peridotite of density 3.1×10^3 kg m^{-3}, then according to the infinite slab formula (equation 2.4) a massive Bouguer gravity increase of 75 mGal results, much as observed along the HMSP section.

3.1.3 Refraction seismology in the Midland Valley

The Scottish Midland Valley is an area of special interest in this Course, so, as in Section 2.3.2 where we examined potential field evidence for concealed intrusions, here we introduce seismic evidence bearing on the shallow crustal structure of this exotic terrane. Seismic refraction data come from three main sources: LISPB, quarry blasts recorded along short profiles, and from the **LOWNET** (the **Lowlands Seismological Network**), which is a widespread network of continuously recording seismometers (marked on Figure 2.18a) that detects natural earthquakes associated with active fault structures around the Midland Valley. Figure 3.12a gives a detailed enlargement of the 3-layer shallow velocity structure across the Midland Valley as determined by LISPB (compare Figure 3.8). This is summarized in the form of a velocity-depth profile in Figure 3.12b together with similar information from LOWNET and the velocity fields for likely lithological groups. These are based on physical property determinations for surface rocks, corrected for the effects of burial.

What are the main differences in the velocity–depth profiles based on LISPB and LOWNET data?

The LOWNET observations resolve a 1 km thick upper layer of velocity 3 km s^{-1}, whereas the LISPB data record a 2–3 km thick upper layer of velocity 4.5–5 km s^{-1}. Layer 2 also has a slightly higher velocity on LISPB than on LOWNET observations.

The differences between the two merely reflect the way the data were collected, along a single line with better resolution at intermediate to deep crustal levels by LISPB, and along several short lines with good shallow resolution in the case of LOWNET. Silurian and Lower Old Red Sandstone lithologies (labelled 72–75 on the Ten Mile Map) occur at the surface both in the north and south of the Midland Valley and may well be an important component of the uppermost 3 km as suggested by the layer 1 data from LISPB. On the other hand, Carboniferous sediments and lavas (labelled 80–83 and 53–55), together with Old Sandstone lavas (labelled 50), form the majority of the surface outcrop in the centre of the Midland Valley, but may only be about 1 km thick, as defined by LOWNET data.

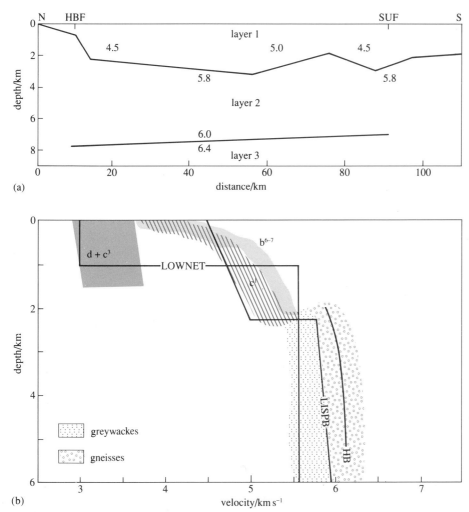

Figure 3.12 (a) Enlargement of the LISPB seismic velocity structure across the Midland Valley of Scotland: HBF, Highland Boundary Fault; SUF, Southern Uplands Fault. (b) Velocity–depth relations for Midland Valley lithological groups as compared with data from LISPB, LOWNET and the Hillhouse–Broughton seismic line (HB—see later in text and Figure 3.13b). d, Carboniferous; c^3, Upper Old Red Sandstone; c^1, Lower Old Red Sandstone; b^{6-7}, Silurian.

Even better resolution of these layers has been obtained from the short refraction profiles using quarry blasts shown in Figure 3.13. The first line (Figure 3.13a, marked as line 1 in Figure 2.18a) runs roughly W–E across the central Midland Valley and has been interpreted as showing four layers. A 1–1.5 km thick layer of Carboniferous sediments (velocity 3.6 km s^{-1}) overlies a wedge of Carboniferous lavas (4.5 km s^{-1}) and a 1–1.5 km thick layer of Lower Old Red Sandstone sediments (5.4 km s^{-1}). At the base of this sequence, there is a strong refractor at 3 km depth beneath which the velocity is c. 6 km s^{-1}. The refractor was traced along about 30 km of this profile, but is probably more extensive, this length being the maximum that can be seen on a 40 km refraction line.

How do these results compare with those of the 80 km long W–E refraction line across the south of the Midland Valley (marked as line 2 in Figure 2.18a) shown in Figure 3.13b?

In the west, a similar Carboniferous–Old Red Sandstone sequence overlies the strong refractor at 2 km depth. East of the Inchgotrick Fault, an uplifted, expanded Old Red Sandstone sequence, including lavas, overlies Silurian sediments. This sequence is upturned towards the centre of the section, bringing Silurian rocks to the surface, in contrast to line 1 where these lithologies are not included. At this point the 6 km s^{-1} refractor is at 3 km depth, as in line 1. There is then a shallow Lower Old Red Sandstone basin and, at the eastern end of the section, the Carmichael Fault brings Old Red Sandstone lavas back into the easternmost outcrop of the Midland

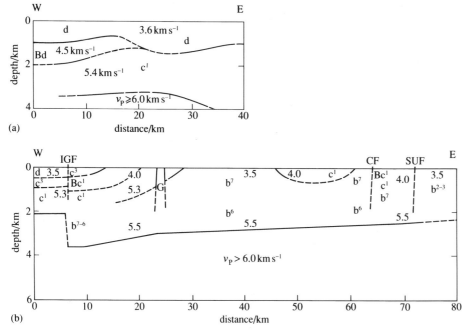

Figure 3.13 Velocity structure beneath two short 'quarry blast' west–east seismic lines across parts of the Midland Valley (locations are as marked in Figure 2.18a):

(a)   Line 1 runs between Glasgow and Edinburgh, crossing the Bathgate potential field anomalies.

(b)   Line 2 is located 30 km further south, and crosses the Southern Uplands Fault (SUF) at its eastern end. IGF is the Inchgotrick fault, CF the Carmichael Fault, and G the Distinkhorn granite.
Lithological groups are as indicated in Figure 3.12 with the addition of Bd, Carboniferous lavas; Bc^l, Lower Old Red Sandstone lavas; b^{2-3}, Ordovician sediments.

Valley, and across the Southern Uplands Fault these are replaced by Ordovician sediments. The 3 km deep strong refractor appears to continue across the Southern Uplands Fault.

These short refraction lines give us considerable confidence that the Silurian to Carboniferous sequence of the Midland Valley is equivalent to the uppermost, superficial (a_s) layer of LISPB (Figure 3.12a) and can be modelled in detail down to 2–3 km depth. But what about the upper crustal layer, beneath the strong refractor, which was labelled as Lower Palaeozoics (a_0) on the preliminary LISPB interpretation (Figure 3.8)?

LOWNET data indicate that this layer is slower (5.5 km s^{-1}) than suggested by LISPB (Figure 3.12a), whereas the short refraction lines indicate higher velocities (≥ 6.0 km s^{-1}; note that the line marked HB in Figure 3.12b is the Hillhouse–Broughton seismic line which you have just considered in Figure 3.13b). As indicated in Figure 3.12b, the lower velocities cover the field of possible velocities for Ordovician greywackes, as found in the Southern Uplands (5.5–5.9 km s^{-1}). The well-constrained higher velocities obtained for the second layer from the short refraction lines (Figure 3.13) have led to the view that *the a_0 layer is not a thick Lower Palaeozoic sequence, but, instead, is composed of high-density, high-grade metamorphic gneisses.* This interpretation fits well with our conclusion (Section 2.3.1) that shallow high-density crystalline basement may underlie the Midland Valley, in order to account for the Bouguer gravity high across this region (cf. also Section 3.1.2) and with the evidence of acid–intermediate gneiss xenoliths that occur in the Carboniferous volcanic vents of the Midland Valley (Block 2).

We hope you agree that these conclusions about the deep structure of the Midland Valley are really quite exciting. There are just two more points arising from the data in Figures 3.12 and 3.13. First, there is no evidence for a shallow source for the potential field anomalies at Bathgate, which is crossed around the centre of line 1. Thus, if the anomalies are due to a Carboniferous basic magmatic vent, as we suspected in Section 2.3.2, *the main part of this source must lie at least 3 km deep within the a_0 layer, or deeper.* Second, the available refraction data from the Midland Valley do not amplify our knowledge of the a_1 layer and deeper lithologies. However, the $6.4 \, \text{km s}^{-1}$ layer that starts at 7–8 km depth is often associated elsewhere with the change from amphibolite to granulite facies metamorphism. Therefore, it is possible that the a_1 layer beneath the Midland Valley comprises granulites (cf. Table 3.1), a suggestion again supported by xenoliths in Carboniferous vents (details in Block 2).

Summary

1   This Section has been entirely concerned with refraction seismology and its use in defining the velocity structure of the lithosphere in Britain. We started by revising the basic principles of refraction seismology, including equations relating the critical angle for refraction to layer velocities (3.1), for determining the thickness of the upper layer using layer velocities and the cross-over distance (3.2) and for interpreting reduced time–distance graphs (3.3 and 3.4).

2   An important distinction was drawn between the propagation of seismic energy along advancing *wave fronts* and the '*rays*' that are used to model wave paths, at right angles to the wave fronts (Figure 3.4).

3   Three important long seismic refraction profiles were discussed in Section 3.1.2. The most important, LISPB, was interpreted in terms of a five layer lithosphere north of the Highland Boundary Fault, comprising a superficial (a_s) layer, upper crustal (a_0 and a_1) layers, a lower crustal (e, f) layer and the upper mantle (c, d) layer—see Table 3.1. This structure appears to continue with some thickness variations beneath the Midland Valley (Figure 3.8). Only the uppermost three layers were identified, unambiguously, south of the Southern Uplands Fault, so that a major break in lithosphere structure occurs in the vicinity of this fault. The Iapetus Suture was not identified by LISPB.

4   The CSSP project provided much improved detail of the velocity structure across northern England, and, although five lithospheric layers were recognized, the two uppermost (a_s and a_0) layers are extremely thin as compared with their LISPB thickness in northern Scotland. Moreover CSSP identified a 13 km thick major upper crustal a_1 layer ($6.15 \, \text{km s}^{-1}$) in northern England, much thicker than on LISPB, together with a lower crustal $6.6 \, \text{km s}^{-1}$ layer and a well-defined Moho at 30 km depth. There is some debate about the geological interpretation of the thick a_1 layer—on the one hand it may be pre-Caledonian basement, for which there is little geological evidence in northern England, while, on the other hand, it may be metamorphosed Lower Palaeozoic volcaniclastics (cf. similar debate about the thinner layer 2 beneath the Midland Valley in Section 3.1.3).

5   HMSP located a gradational transition from continental to oceanic lithosphere west of the Hebridean craton in which crustal thickness decreased from 27 to 18 km along a 100 km part of the seismic line. True oceanic lithosphere with a *c.* 8 km thick oceanic crust is presumed to lie further west.

6   LISPB, LOWNET and quarry blast short refraction lines across the Midland Valley have been used to model the upper crust in detail (Section 3.1.3), revealing: (i) a 2–3 km thick Silurian to Carboniferous sequence (termed a_s on LISPB), beneath which there is (ii) a strong refractor due to velocities in the second layer exceeding $6.0 \, \text{km s}^{-1}$. This layer is thought to be composed of high-density, high-grade metamorphosed gneisses rather than Lower Palaeozoics (note that this is the a_0 layer in the Midland Valley, whereas a thicker layer—defined as a_1—of similar velocity but inferred from gravity data to be of lower density was identified by CSSP—see 4 above). (iii) A $6.4 \, \text{km s}^{-1}$ granulite layer was found extending from 8 to 20 km depth (the a_1 layer—note the strong contrast with CSSP, where the probable Lower Palaeozoic a_1 layer extends from 3–17 km depth).

3.2 REFLECTION SEISMOLOGY

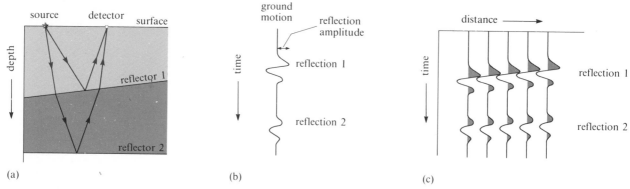

Figure 3.14 Seismic reflection, traces and sections: (a) illustrates reflection from two reflectors with fixed source and detector producing: (b) a seismic trace with two reflected arrivals at different times (note the reflection amplitude for reflection 1); (c) a seismic section built up from series of 5 traces moving from left to right across the dipping reflector in (a) and involving a series of 5 shot-points with the positive parts of each trace shaded.

In the seismic reflection method, elastic waves, generated at or near the surface, travel through the ground until they reach a boundary at which they are reflected, return to the surface and are recorded (Figure 3.14a). The record of ground motion with time on land, or of pressure pulses transmitted by the water in marine surveys, is called a **seismic trace** (Figure 3.14b, which illustrates the two reflections resulting from Figure 3.14a). Notice that the angle of incidence at each boundary is equal to the angle of reflection. The amplitude of a reflection signal, the **reflection amplitude**, is the deviation of the trace from a straight line and gives a measure of the strength of ground motion (or pressure pulse). Notice, in contrast to the travel-time diagrams of refraction seismology, convention in reflection work is to plot time increasing downwards. If several seismic traces from adjacent locations are displayed side by side, we obtain a **seismic section**. (Figure 3.14c), which gives a clear impression that the upper interface or **reflector** in Figure 3.14a is dipping, because reflected arrivals from this interface take progressively less time to the right. In order to emphasize strong arrivals from a prominent reflector, a common convention in reflection seismology is to shade in the positive or compressional parts of each trace as shown in Figure 3.14c. In this way, important reflecting horizons on the seismic sections show up as prominent dark bands with white areas beneath, due to the succeeding negative, dilatational parts of the seismic waves.

An example of the end result of the method is shown in Figure 3.15. The horizontal scale is distance, to which **shot-point (SP)** locations and numbers can be related. There are 1 600 shot-points on this section—little wonder, then, that you cannot distinguish each seismic trace!

In this particular case, the shot-points were 25 m apart, so how wide is the seismic section?

1 600 × 25 = 40 000 m, or 40 km. You should add a distance scale across the top of Figure 3.15.

The vertical scale is measured in **two-way time (TWT)**, which is the time taken for the seismic waves to travel down into the ground and back up again after reflection. We have given approximate depths on this section based on estimated upper crustal velocities (increasing downwards—hence the downwards compression of the depth scale), and this reveals that the entire section has a vertical exaggeration of around 4:1.

How is such a seismic section interpreted? The primary requirement is to seek **reflection continuity**, where a prominent reflection is recognized on many adjacent traces. Take the strong reflector at just over 2 s TWT on the right-hand side of Figure 3.15; it is particularly prominent between SP 600 and 1200 but then fades and loses continuity around SP 1800. Clearly, seismic reflection methods are particularly

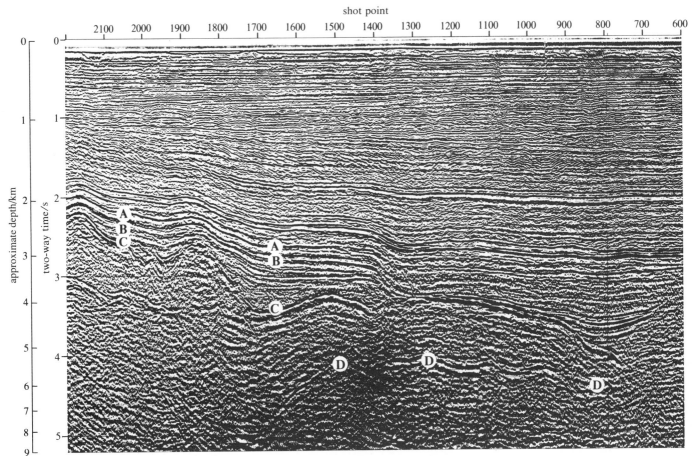

Figure 3.15 A seismic section from the Central Graben in the North Sea. The major stratigraphic units shown are: A, base of Tertiary; B, top of Lower Cretaceous; C, base of Lower Cretaceous; D, top of Triassic.

well suited to the mapping of sedimentary sequences such as those represented in the shallower parts of Figure 3.15. But what about areas such as between SP 1800 and 2200 at > 4 s TWT where there is no reflection continuity? There are several possible reasons for this lack of continuity; the area may have no reflecting interfaces, too complex a structure, or, simply, there may be insufficient seismic energy to resolve the geological detail present.

In addition to layering, seismic sections provide good information for structural mapping, and it is here that their value has recently been proved in deep lithospheric studies of the type we shall be considering. In particular, it is possible to recognize faults, folds, unconformities and other structures.

> **ITQ 3.5** Interpreting seismic sections at a qualitative level is really quite easy: try to find an example of an anticline, a syncline, and if you can, a fault and an unconformity in Figure 3.15.

Remember that the vertical exaggeration of seismic sections such as Figure 3.15 (in this case 4:1) makes the faults appear much more vertical than they really are. Note also that the apparent fold structures present are not necessarily the product of compressional deformation. In the cases considered here, they may be partly due to differential compaction above deep faults and partly due to the draping of syn-depositional sediments over the evolving fault-block topography.

There are several other features in Figure 3.15 that are not quite so easy to interpret, the dipping reflections around 1.5 s TWT for example, and the disappearance of the prominent reflection around 3.5 s between SP 600 and SP 700. The interpretation of these features will become clearer as you read on. But remember that in this Course we are most interested in the results of geophysical surveys for the interpretation of deep lithosphere structure. We shall therefore not be considering seismic reflection data acquisition and processing in *great* detail.

3.2.1 Reflection seismic data interpretation: some basic principles

First, a note of caution. You will have begun to realize that a seismic section is rather like a slice through the Earth. But, although seismic sections do show the general features of the geology, they are definitely not geological sections. The main difference is that the true *vertical scale is in units of time, not depth*. Of course, seismic wave velocities increase with depth so seismic sections tend to be expanded near the top and compressed near the bottom compared with true depth sections (cf. left-hand axis of Figure 3.15). The conversion process from time to depth is expensive, and is usually unnecessary when concentrating on structural detail.

Another fundamental assumption is that reflection takes place from a geological horizon, whereas the true nature of a seismic reflector is that it is a boundary, or interface, for example between contrasting strata, across fault planes, etc. In fact, prominent reflections arise at an interface if there is a contrast in the physical property known as the **acoustic impedance** of the rocks adjacent to the interface. Acoustic impedance (z) is defined as:

$$z = \rho v \, \mathrm{kg\,m^{-2}\,s^{-1}} \tag{3.5}$$

where ρ is the density and v the p-wave velocity. If the acoustic impedances either side of a geological boundary are the same, no reflection will occur. But note that reflection may occur at a boundary between rock layers with the same velocities if the densities, and therefore the acoustic impedances, are different. Reflection amplitude depends on the contrast in acoustic impedance across the boundary, and is more normally considered in terms of the ratio of the amplitude of the reflected wave to that of the incident wave, known as the **reflection coefficient** (R):

$$R = \frac{z_2 - z_1}{z_2 + z_1} \tag{3.6}$$

This equation is valid for a wave incident at right angles to the interface ($i=0°$); R generally increases as the angle of incidence increases, reaching a maximum at and beyond the critical angle (where none of the incident energy is refracted). However, you should remember that a reflected wave will occur only when there is a change in acoustic impedance across the interface; if $R=0$ in equation 3.6 there is no reflected wave. Reflection coefficients are mostly less than 0.05, giving weak reflections, and nearly always less than 0.1. Those between 0.1 and 0.2 give very strong reflections, and a reflection coefficient exceeding 0.2 would give an exceptionally strong reflection on a seismic section.

> **ITQ 3.6** What strength of reflection would you expect from the following geological interfaces (use average ρ and mean velocity data from Table 2.1):
>
> (a)   An intrusive contract between granite and limestone;
>
> (b)   Rhyolite lava flow within a shale sequence;
>
> (c)   A faulted contact between granulite and shales.

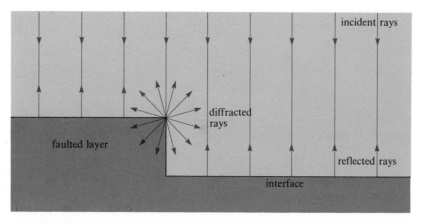

Figure 3.16 Diffraction is the scattering of seismic energy caused by terminations or sharp curves on an interface. In this case, only vertically directed seismic wave paths and reflections are shown, except where there is a sharp boundary on the interface where a new variety of wave paths results in hyperbolic reflection arrivals on seismic sections (Figures 3.17 and 3.18).

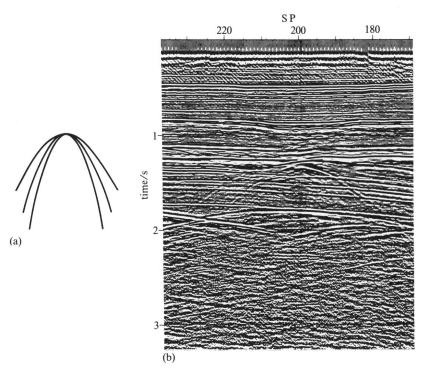

Figure 3.17 (a) Hyperbolic shapes. Each hyperbola has its apex at the same point. (b) Diffraction hyperbolae on a seismic section. The apex of the hyperbolae is at SP 200, 1.3 s and is probably caused by undulations on the interface marked by the strong reflections just above this depth.

The normal principles of reflection and refraction apply to interfaces that are continuous and flat, or have only a low curvature. If an interface terminates abruptly, or is very curved, the incident energy is scattered in all directions. This scattering of a wave is called **diffraction** and is illustrated in Figure 3.16. Generally, it is easy to recognize diffractions on a seismic section because they produce very distinctive hyperbolic shapes (Figure 3.17). The tails of the **diffraction hyperbolae** usually fade away at depth. Diffractions may initially seem just a nuisance, as they may obscure parts of the reflection section available for geological interpretation. But they can be quite useful, for example in tracing the position of a fault as the apices (tops) of diffraction hyperbolae often align with a fault plane. However, as you can see from Figure 3.18a, the diffractions produced by the terminations of sedimentary layers at a fault plane dipping gently to the right have the effect of obscuring the reflections to either side, so fault diffractions are a mixed blessing!

> You may have noticed that the fault plane traced by the diffraction hyperbolae in Figure 3.18a is rather curved. Why might this occur, given that faults are usually planar structures?

This is a good example of the effect on seismic sections of increasing velocity with depth. If a constant near-surface velocity is assumed, then the position of deep reflectors, where part of the wave path has been at a higher velocity than assumed, will appear at a shallower depth on a seismic section than on a true geological section (Figures 3.18b and c).

So far, we have talked only of wave paths that are vertical, but as you will appreciate from the comments above about reflection coefficient, more reflected energy is available if the angle of incidence at an interface is increased, particularly if this exceeds the critical angle (cf. Figure 3.2). The usual practice in reflection surveying is to record each shot with many detector groups (usually 24, 48 or 96) at various horizontal distances from the shot: this is called **multichannel reflection profiling**. This technique has the advantage of improving the signal to noise ratio by obtaining many reflections for every point on each reflecting boundary (i.e. on each reflector). The way in which the resulting seismic traces are put together will be described shortly.

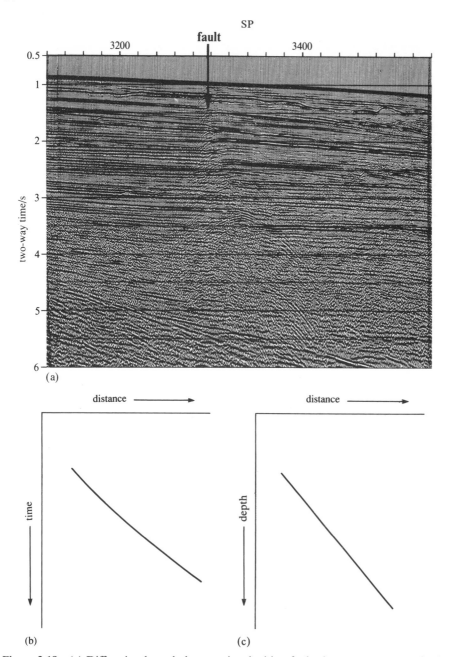

Figure 3.18 (a) Diffraction hyperbolae associated with a fault plane as seen on a seismic section; (b) The appearance of a fault plane trace on a seismic reflection section where velocity increases with depth. This has the effect of foreshortening the apparent position of the fault (i.e. it appears more shallow) as compared with its true geological position (c).

There are two common source/detector geometries, the **split spread** and the **end spread** (Figure 3.19), and in neither case is it necessary to move all the detectors between successive shots. In the split spread, the detectors are laid out in a line on either side of the shot point and the next shot might be at the position of detector 7, so only detectors 7 and 14 must be moved to reproduce the same configuration at the next shot point. Split spreads and end spreads are equally convenient for use on land whereas only the end spread is appropriate for use at sea, where all the equipment is towed behind the ship—which travels at constant speed and shots are fired at regular intervals. As you will appreciate, in neither case are the wave paths vertical, so how are different signals combined to produce a seismic trace relating to each shot point so that these can be incorporated into a seismic section?

Use is made of the fact that several traces from *each* point on the reflector are produced by successive shots. For example, in Figure 3.19a, reflections from point X are recorded by detector 1 but not by any others during that shot. However, when the shot point has moved to the left, reflections from X will be recorded (through

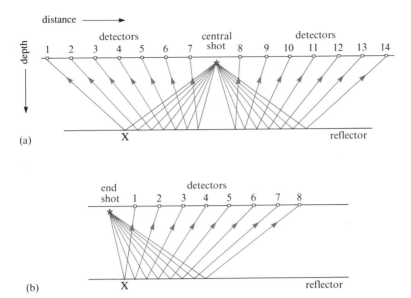

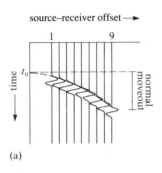

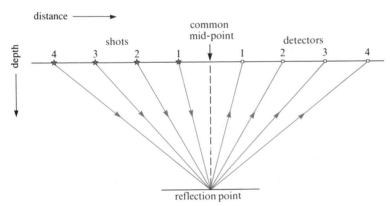

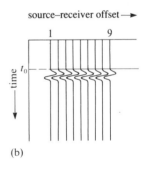

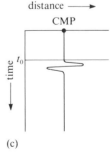

Figure 3.19 (a) Split spread and (b) end spread multichannel surveys on land.

Figure 3.20 Cartoon of the geometry of common mid-point surveys in which reflections from the same point (vertically below the common mid-point) occur for each shot-detector pair (1, 2, 3, 4, etc.).

smaller angles of incidence and reflection) at detector 2, and so on, as illustrated in Figure 3.20. Notice now that all the signals (reaching detectors 1–4 in Figure 3.20) arise from a point *vertically below the mid-point* between each shot-detector pair known as the **common mid-point (CMP)**. The next stage is to take each of the many records relating to a particular point on the reflector (four records in the case of Figure 3.20), and to correct them for their different travel lengths and times to the reflector. So the travel times are adjusted by computer to the **zero-offset travel time** (t_0), which gives the times to different reflectors that would have been recorded if the detector and source were both at the CMP. The necessary adjustment is called the **normal moveout correction (NMO)**, and the phenomenon shown in Figure 3.21a is a normal moveout. This process of NMO correction takes us from Figure 3.21a to Figure 3.21b; finally, all the time-corrected traces are added together, a process known as **stacking**, to obtain a single seismic trace for the mid-point (Figure 3.21c). Just to emphasize the point: the stacked trace is what would have been recorded if detector and source were both at the CMP, with vertical reflected wave paths. As you will now appreciate, this improves the quality of the signal and diminishes any 'noise' not due to genuine reflections. Stacking is, not surprisingly, the single most important stage in seismic data processing. Nevertheless, many other computer-based methods are employed to improve the quality of the final seismic section; all apart from migration (see below) are beyond the scope of this Course.

Look again at Figure 3.20, and try to imagine what would happen if the reflector was not horizontal.

Figure 3.21 (a) Change in time with distance for nine sets of arrivals about a common mid-point (as in Figure 3.20). 1 is the trace from shot 1 recorded on detector 1, etc. (b) Normal moveout corrections are applied by computer so that all travel times are as if there were zero offset (i.e. shot and detector both vertically above the reflection point.) (c) The nine corrected traces are stacked to produce a single trace for this mid-point.

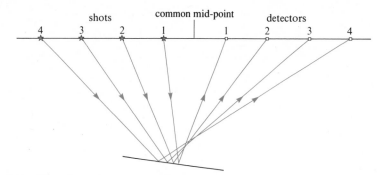

Figure 3.22 The effect of a dipping reflector is that the reflection points no longer occur beneath the common mid-point (*cf.* Figure 3.20).

The answer is shown in Figure 3.22—the reflection point on a dipping reflector is no longer below the CMP and no more is it a constant point for different source–detector pairs.

The objective of seismic data **migration** is to move the dipping reflectors from their apparent position, as mapped directly beneath the CMP, to their correct spatial location, thus building up a true image of the reflector. Before you get confused, please note that migration is a quite different and much more complex computational process than correcting time sections for true depth—cf. Figure 3.18—and migrated sections will still show planar dipping surfaces as curved if velocity increases downwards.

> Now look again carefully at Figure 3.22. Where will the reflection point be plotted on a seismic section relative to its true position on the reflector—up-dip or down-dip?

The answer is down-dip—the reflection point will plot as though it was vertically beneath the CMP, between shot-point 1 and detector 1, whereas its true position is somewhere beneath shot-point 1 in this example. To illustrate this point more fully, consider the signals received at CMP point A in Figure 3.23a. They actually come from point X on the reflector, but will be displayed on the stacked, zero offset time-corrected seismic section at Y, where YA = XA in travel time. Compared with its true position at X, therefore, the reflection point is moved down-dip to Y on the seismic section. The same process has affected the other points shown in Figure 3.23a, and the overall effect is to make the *dip of the interface on the section less than it should be*. In this case, the true dip is α and the apparent dip on the section is β.

> Use the construction in Figure 3.23b to find a geometric relationship between the angles α and β: first write down expressions for $\sin \alpha$ and $\tan \beta$.

> In the triangle OAX, with a right angle at X, $\sin \alpha = AX/OA$

> In the triangle OAY, with a right angle at A, $\tan \beta = AY/OA$

> Since $AX = AY$, the relationship must be

$$\sin \alpha = \tan \beta \tag{3.7}$$

You might realize, on examining this equation, that it will break down when $\beta > 45°$, because the tangent of angles greater than 45° exceeds unity, for which there are no sine values. What this is telling us is that on a seismic section with a true 1:1 vertical to horizontal scaling, no reflectors can appear to dip at an angle greater than 45°, i.e. the steepest possible reflector (just less than 90° dip) produces an unmigrated reflection dipping at almost 45°. This emphasizes the importance of migration! Advantages of migration other than its value in producing true dip seismic sections with structures in their correct horizontal position are (a) that the process tends to clean up diffractions (i.e. they 'collapse' to a single point), and (b) that the true widths of anticlinal and synclinal structures are revealed (anticlines appear wider and synclines narrower in seismic sections than they really are). The main aim of the seismic sections we shall be examining in the remainder of this Block is to reveal

ie reflections will not be recorded from reflections with steep dips.

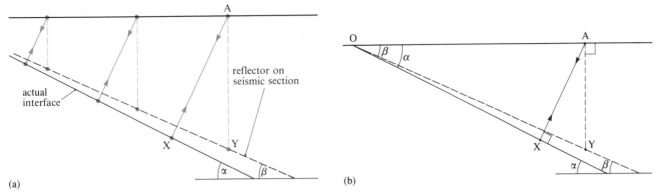

Figure 3.23   (a) A dipping interface and its position on a seismic section (dashed black line). A reflection from point X on the interface is shifted to point Y on the seismic section. The true dip of the interface (α) is greater than the dip of the interface on the seismic section (β). The correction applied to produce true time-distance dips on a seismic section is known as migration. (b) Construction as in (a) projected back to the surface in order to determine the relationship between α and β.

faults and thrusts down to 40–50 km, so migration can be very important in finding their correct vertical and horizontal positions. Many of these have been migrated and some have also been converted through the final step of data processing into depth sections.

In this section, we have covered the basic principles needed for you to understand the seismic sections that follow at a qualitative structural level. There is one final point to make about data interpretation, and that concerns **seismic modelling**, which you will shortly see illustrated in the video programme. This technique involves producing a geological model, perhaps based on borehole data, or independent geophysical data, from which reflection times can be calculated and compared with those observed. In detail, as in refraction seismology, *ray tracing* techniques are used in conjunction with the geological model, and, from the travel time information produced, synthetic seismic traces are generated. In turn, these traces can be combined to produce a **synthetic seismic section** (e.g. Figure 3.24), which can be compared with the original. The model is then iteratively adjusted to reduce any discrepancies until an acceptable correspondence is achieved. Nevertheless, the determination of seismic velocities from reflection data alone is ambiguous.

3.2.2 Seismic reflection profiling of Britain: general features

Until quite recently, most seismic reflection investigations into the structure of the continental lithosphere were based on-shore, in the USA, Australia, Europe and the USSR. But Britain's extensive continental shelf made off-shore data collection an attractive alternative, especially as it is faster and therefore cheaper to collect, and generally gives data of higher quality.

> Why do you think off-shore seismic reflection data is often of better quality than on-shore data?

At sea, where explosions are detonated beneath the water surface, very little seismic energy is lost to the atmosphere and so signals with a higher reflection amplitude can be obtained. Ambient noise also tends to be lower at sea, so a better signal to noise ratio is available. Also, the sea is a repeatable medium in which to place the source and receivers, whereas, on land, the local structure is very variable from shot to shot. However, there are disadvantages, the most significant being that off-shore geology is less well known than that on-shore, making interpretation more speculative. Nevertheless, the off-shore seismic reflection profiling programme around Britain, initiated in 1981 by **BIRPS**, based round a core group at Cambridge University, is one of the most ambitious geophysical investigations ever undertaken. BIRPS, the acronym stands for the **British Institutions' Reflection Profiling Syndicate**, has made excellent use of the technological developments of the 1950–1980 period in data acquisition and processing to generate (by 1989) over 12 000 km of high quality seismic reflection profiles, more than a quarter of the world's deep seismic reflection data (Figure 3.25). The major achievement has been a consistent ability to image

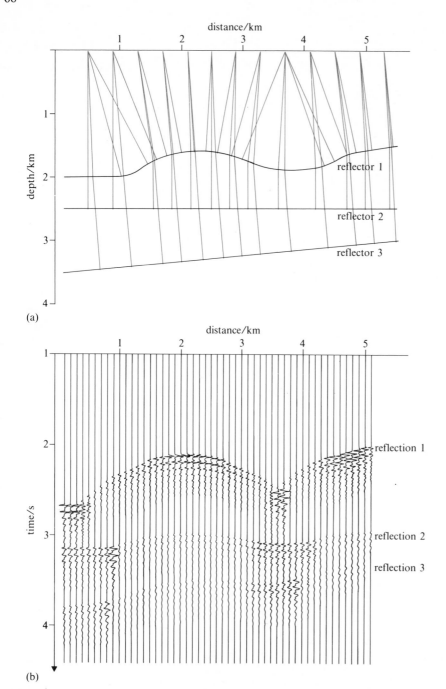

(a)

(b)

Figure 3.24 (a) Geological model, with the seismic ray paths to three reflectors. Notice that the model is a distance–depth section constructed by interpreting a seismic section of distance against TWT. The known or estimated physical properties of each layer are used to create the model, which is then tested (b) by constructing a synthetic seismic section for comparison with that originally observed.

structures in the lower crust and upper mantle, enabling rheological and modelling studies to progress concerning the ductility and strength of the crust at the continental scale. We shall touch on these at the end of this Block (Section 3.2.5) and again more fully in Block 5. Other significant discoveries have included tracing suture zones across Britain, allowing geological models to be constructed of terrane accretion processes. We shall examine these in the context of the Iapetus Suture and the Hercynian Front in Sections 3.2.3 and 3.2.4 using data from the NEC and SWAT profiles (Figure 3.25).

Clearly, time and space do not allow us to describe all the BIRPS lines in detail, interesting as this might be. So by way of introduction to the general features, in this Section we shall consider parts of just three lines, among the first to be acquired and processed by BIRPS: the MOIST, WINCH and DRUM lines adjacent to the north

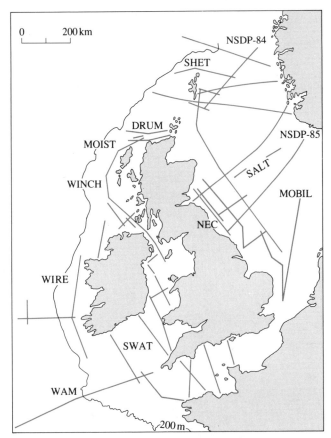

Figure 3.25 Deep seismic reflection profiles obtained mainly by the British Institutions' Reflection Profiling Syndicate (BIRPS) during the 1980s. NSDP, North Sea Deep Profiles; SHET, Shetland Profile; DRUM, Deep Reflections from the Upper Mantle; MOIST, Moine and Outer Isles Seismic Traverse; WINCH, Western Isles, North Channel profile; NEC, North East Coast profile; SALT (no acronym, recorded over salt diapirs in the North Sea); SWAT, South West Approaches Traverse; WAM, Western Approaches Margin profile; WIRE, West of Ireland; MOBIL, Measurements Over Basins to Image the Lithosphere.

and northwest coast of Scotland. To simplify matters for the moment, we present these data as *line drawings*, produced by tracing coherent reflections from the seismic section (there is an example of both in Figures 3.28a and b if you would like to see a comparison). In this form, the data are more easily displayed and interpreted, but a loss of detail is an inevitable consequence. At the scale of these sections, it is usual to assume crust and mantle velocities of 6 and $8\,\mathrm{km\,s^{-1}}$ respectively, so TWT multiplied by 3 in the crust and by 4 in the mantle will give *approximate* depths.

Figure 3.26 gives such line diagrams for the three seismic reflection profiles around northern Scotland, and you should note the following points:

(i)   The MOIST data (Figure 3.26a) are a synthesis of the main reflectors prepared from unmigrated seismic sections of this 175 km line.

(ii)   A location map for the WINCH data is given in Figure 3.26b, and the data in Figures 3.26c–e arise, respectively, from the 120 km long section BC, north of Lewis, and the 200 km long sections CD and DE along the western margin of Scotland. These are unmigrated data. We shall look at EF in relation to the Iapetus Suture in Section 3.2.3.

(iii)   The DRUM data (Figure 3.26f) refer to a second 175 km line run parallel to MOIST just to the north of Scotland; again this line diagram was prepared from unmigrated data, but the remarkable achievement of the DRUM profile was that records from 30 s TWT were collected, representing lithosphere depths of 100 km. (Most other BIRPS lines are recorded to 15 s TWT and 'see' down to about 50 km, well into the upper mantle, itself a major bonus, considering that very few mantle reflectors have been recognized anywhere else in the world. Notice the compressed vertical scale in Figure 3.26f compared with the other line diagrams, which are almost true scale in the crust.)

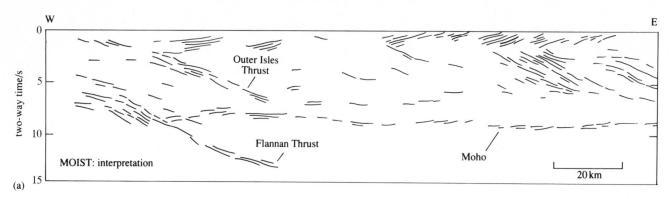

W   E

MOIST: interpretation

(a)

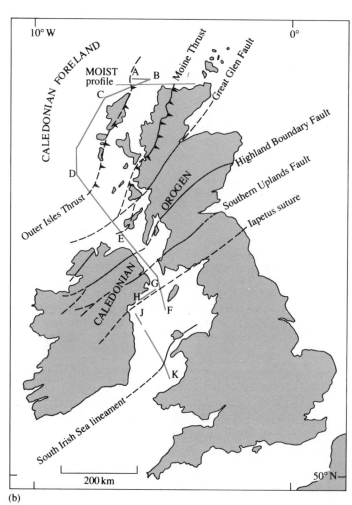

(b)

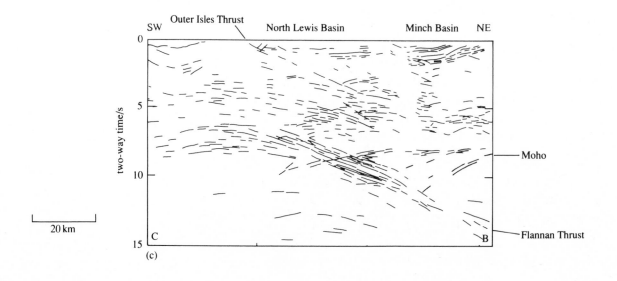

(c)

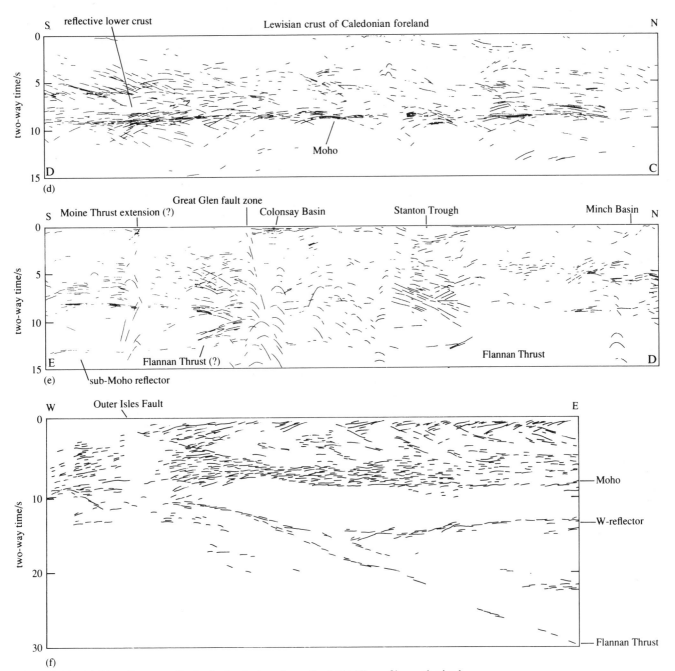

Figure 3.26 (a) Line diagram of principal reflectors from the MOIST profile synthesized from migrated and unmigrated data. (b) Location map for the WINCH profile segments with respect to the Caledonian foreland, orogen and major Caledonian faults. (c) to (e) Line diagrams of unmigrated WINCH data in segments B to E around northern and western Scotland (note that north is to the right of these sections). (f) Line diagram of unmigrated DRUM line off north Scotland—see Figure 3.25 for location. Note that (a) and (c) to (e) are approximately true scale (i.e. vertical = horizontal) in the crust where the velocity is *c*. 6 km s⁻¹. The vertical scale is compressed by a factor of about two-thirds in diagram (f).

The Upper Crust

ITQ 3.7 Examine the line drawings of the BIRPS profiles shown in Figure 3.26, and try to describe the main reflection seismic features of the upper crust (i) from 0 to 1.5 s TWT and (ii) from 1.5 to 4 s TWT.

Not surprisingly, the shallow sets of parallel reflections are due to sedimentary layering in basins that extend to 3–4 km depth. For example, you may recall the gravity low associated with the Minch Basin, between the Outer Hebrides and mainland Scotland (Block 1A, Figure 3.20). The northern and southern extensions of this basin, crossed by the WINCH line near B and D, produce reflections down to 1.5 s TWT, equivalent to 4 km depth. Smaller but more prominent basins in reflection terms occur on the MOIST and DRUM lines; these contain known sedimentary sequences mainly of Devonian and younger age. Rather than being symmetrical basins, many of these are 'half-grabens' related to earlier east–west thrusts that are thought to have extended by rotation on curved or parallel sets of normal faults (Figure 3.27, cf. also Block 1A, Figure 3.13). The repeated half-grabens, all with sedimentary layering dipping west on the MOIST and DRUM lines, suggest a kind of domino effect, where a series of parallel fault blocks have extended (cf. Block 1A, Figures 2.15, 3.12) perhaps on one side of a major basin, in this case the North Sea. (Of course, the majority of the extension in the North Sea area took place in the Mesozoic, whereas Palaeozoic extension is a feature of the seismic sections north of Scotland). Beneath this shallow sedimentary layer, apart from the easterly-dipping faults just described, most of the upper crust produces very few reflections—it is said to be **seismically transparent**. This transparency may be a fundamental characteristic of the upper crust, but equally it could be a consequence of the data acquisition and processing methods used, which were designed to enhance deep reflections, with the consequence that shallower reflections may have been degraded.

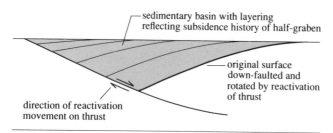

Figure 3.27   Schematic illustration of the formation of a sedimentary half-graben basin due to extension on a deeper fault plane.

The Middle and Lower Crust

> Re-examine the line drawings in Figure 3.26. What is the most striking overall reflection seismic characteristic of the middle and lower crust, from 4 s to 8–9 s TWT?

The middle and lower crust, especially on the WINCH and DRUM lines, are generally characterized by short, sub-horizontal reflections ranging up to 15 km in length. The top of this reflective zone is sharp in some locations but gradational in others. Some of these deep crustal reflections appear to cross each other—in case this was worrying you, this does not mean that we have interpenetrating reflectors, merely that the section (a) is unmigrated, and (b) may be picking up signals out of the plane of section (known as sideswipe). Seismic experiments in southern Britain, the

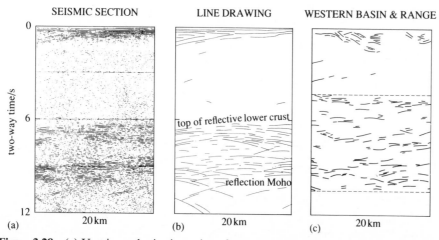

Figure 3.28   (a) Unmigrated seismic section of part of the SWAT profiles from south west Britain showing a prominent Moho at about 10 s TWT overlain by reflective lower crust (6.5–10 s TWT); (b) Line diagram based on the seismic data in (a). (c) Line diagram of reflections from the western Basin and Range Province, USA also showing reflective lower crust, in this case from 4.5 to 10.5 s TWT.

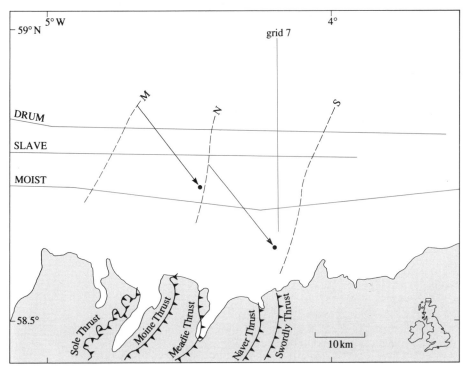

Figure 3.29 Map of the northern Scottish coast showing adjacent deep seismic reflection lines. The positions of major Caledonian thrusts are shown onshore; offshore present-day positions as inferred from seismic data are given by dashed lines: M, Moine Thrust; N, Naver Thrust; S, Swordly Thrust. Fine arrows indicate vectors along which the present-day thrust positions must be moved to restore the late Palaeozoic extensional faulting.

USA, Australia and Germany have defined similarly reflective lower crust (e.g. Figure 3.28), showing that this is not a feature unique to northern Britain. We shall consider the possible reasons for lower crustal reflectivity more fully in Block 5; in brief, the possibilities are: (i) the depth to the top of the reflective layer may be correlated with surface heat flow, and layering may thus be a function of mid-crustal temperatures, and (ii) the origin of the reflectivity is perhaps related to ductile strain-banding produced by earlier deformation under tectonic stress, and/or (iii) it may be due to the intrusion of basic sill-like bodies into the lower crust.

Outer Isles Thrust, Moine Thrust and Great Glen Fault

Some of the easterly-dipping fault reflectors in the upper crust seem to traverse at least part of the lower crust. Notice, in particular, the appearance of the Outer Isles Thrust on all three seismic sections. This is the major structural feature that forms the western boundary of the Minch Basin, and the adjacent North Lewis Basin (Figure 3.26c). It is the most extreme northwesterly fault marked at the surface in Block 1A, Figure 3.20, and we now see that it cuts right through the Lewisian rocks of the Hebridean Craton. So, using reflection seismic techniques, we have been able to identify a major fault structure that traverses almost the entire crust. But does it reach the Moho? Apparently not in the sections given in Figure 3.26, but we shall come back to this soon.

A similar suite of dipping reflectors traverses the entire upper crust at the eastern end of the MOIST profile (Figure 3.26a) and reaches the surface where the profile crosses the Moine Thrust (Block 1A, Figure 3.23). You will recall that one of the disappointing aspects of LISPB was that it failed to image the major faults of northern Scotland; clearly the better resolution reflection data seem to be imaging the Moine Thrust, but exactly which of the reflectors is the main thrust?

The problem is complicated because the Moine Thrust is just one of a series of Caledonian thrusts that occur on-shore. From west to east (Figure 3.29), these are the Sole Thrust, the Moine Thrust, the Meadie, Naver and Swordly Thrusts (but please don't attempt to remember them all!). In a 1990 reinterpretation of the network of reflection data north of Scotland (cf. Figure 3.25), David Snyder of the BIRPS group was able to recognize three main sets of dipping reflectors (Figure

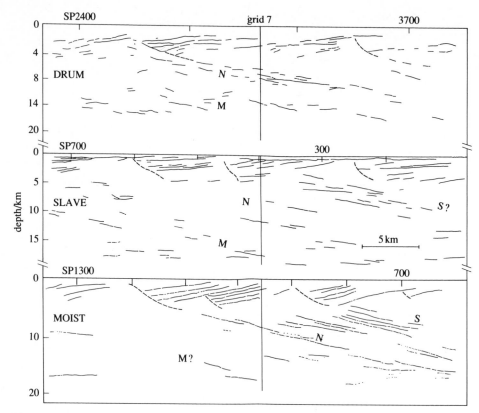

Figure 3.30 Line drawings comparing deep reflection data for the MOIST, SLAVE and DRUM profiles in 40 km wide sections adjacent to the outcrop of the Moine Thrust in northern Scotland. M, N and S are as given in Figure 3.29 and the dashed lines represent the inferred positions of normal faults.

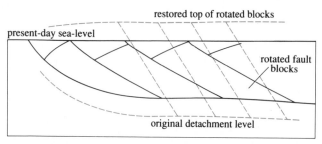

Figure 3.31 Schematic figure to illustrate the rotational displacement of normal fault blocks when restored above a basal detachment plane. Notice how near-surface features move to the right during restoration even though thinning also occurs to the right. The original thickness of the zone above the detachment would, of course, have been greater and restoration shows that the offshore area would have been above sea-level prior to extension, even allowing for isostatic movement of the detachment plane.

3.30). Those due to the Naver and Swordly Thrusts are most prominent, but the Moine Thrust was located beneath, forming the zone at about 18 km depth (TWT *c.* 7 s on Figure 3.26a) into which the more easterly thrusts merge. This is regarded as a major mid-crustal detachment zone, which also provides the root zone to which the upper crustal normal faults, which form the western margins of the sedimentary basins, are connected (cf. Figures 3.27 and 3.30). The only difficulty is that the surface traces of two of the three deep thrusts recognized by Snyder (M and N in Figure 3.29) are located some 20 km west of a continuation of their on-shore positions. If, however, allowance is made for extension to the east and the consequent rotation of the fault blocks (cf. Figure 3.31), we find that the 'restored' (i.e. original, pre-extension) positions of the Moine and Naver Thrusts occur some 20 km further east (actually southeast) of their apparent surface locations today—hence the restoration vectors in Figure 3.29. The full argument is a good deal more detailed than this, of course, but we hope that Figure 3.31 helps you appreciate that Palaeozoic extension off the northern coast of Scotland was responsible (a) for rotating some of the major older thrusts, thus apparently moving their surface traces west, (b) for creating small sedimentary 'half-graben' basins, and

(c) for thinning the upper crust so that the present-day coastline at least partly reflects the boundary between a zone of major Palaeozoic extension (to the north) and less extension (to the south). In summary, the Moine Thrust and several associated Caledonian thrust structures, subsequently reactivated, have been located by seismic reflection techniques.

Finally, the Great Glen Fault, also not imaged by LISPB, has a prominent expression on the WINCH profile (Figure 3.26e) where it is crossed south of Mull.

How would you describe its image on the WINCH seismic section?

It is marked by a near vertical series of prominent diffraction hyperbolae that extend right through the crust. In fact this is mainly energy back-scattered from the sea–sediment interface, where the sea-bottom topography must be influenced by the fault. We know this partly because the dip of the reflections associated with the Great Glen Fault is far too steep on this unmigrated section to represent a real fault structure within the crust (maximum dip on unmigrated sections $= 45°$ from equation 3.7). In fact, the Great Glen Fault appears to be a 10–15 km wide zone south of Mull, and some downthrow on the north side has produced the Colonsay Basin (Figure 3.26e). Remember, of course, that the major movement along this fault is thought, on geological grounds, to have been strike–slip in nature.

The Moho

The visibility of the Moho on the BIRPS profiles (Figure 3.26) is quite variable. On the MOIST and DRUM profiles, it is a clearly defined reflection, or series of reflections at 8–9 s TWT (*c.* 27 km depth)—and high quality reflections are visible in the seismic sections (Figure 3.32). In contrast, along parts of the WINCH profile, it is visible only as the base of the lower crustal reflections. This variation in Moho visibility appears to be unrelated to crustal type: the Moho is equally as clear below the Lewisian foreland as it is beneath the Caledonian orogeny east of the Moine Thrust.

How well does the depth of the Moho in North Scotland on the MOIST, WINCH and DRUM profiles agree with that defined by LISPB?

The LISPB interpretation (Figure 3.8) has the Moho at between 25 and 30 km depth in this region, values remarkably close to the best that we can deduce from the seismic reflection profiles. Indeed, a striking feature of all the BIRPS work is the similarity of Moho reflection times around Britain; while crustal velocities will vary a little from place to place, these variations probably are so small that we can conclude that the *depth* to the Moho around Britain is fairly uniform (25–35 km except for the most recently extended zone in the North Sea graben) and is not affected in any major way by past collisional processes.

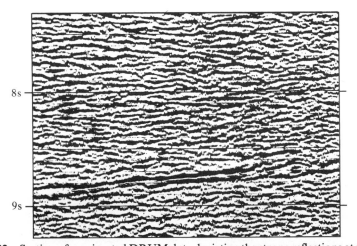

Figure 3.32 Section of unmigrated DRUM data depicting the strong reflections at nearly 9 s TWT due to the Moho.

Deep faults and upper mantle features

We start with another look at the Outer Isles Thrust which was recorded on the short section of the WINCH line marked AB in Figure 3.26b. At the western end of this section (Figures 3.33a and b) we find the westerly-dipping reflectors of the North Lewis Basin which extends, at a maximum to 3.5 s TWT, a remarkable 8 km deep (allowing for low sediment velocities of *c.* 4.5 km s^{-1}). Beneath this basin, the Outer Isles Thrust dips at about 21° to the east.

What is the dip after migration correction?

Using equation 3.7 sin $a = \tan 21° = 0.3839$, so $a = 22.6°$.

So the migration correction steepens the fault by about 1.6°, but what about the effect of the low-velocity sediments? Referring to Figure 3.18b, you can see that the apparent, migrated dip must be steepened even more to produce a true geological dip. A geological model based on synthetic seismic ray tracing (Figure 3.33c) steepens the fault to 29° and introduces an interesting intersection between the Outer

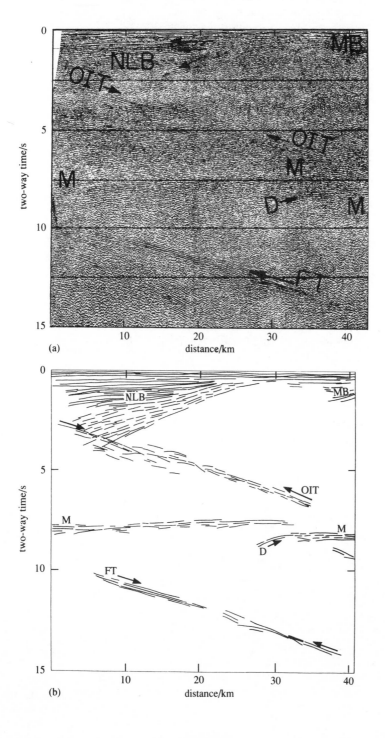

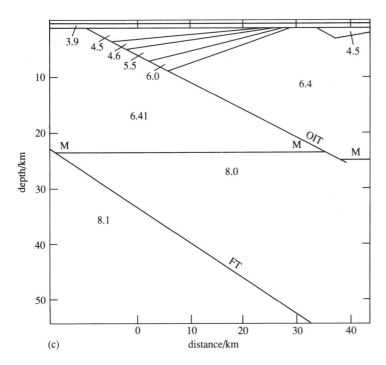

Figure 3.33 (a) WINCH unmigrated section AB off northern Scotland and (b) line diagram illustrating the main features of this section. FT, Flannan Thrust; OIT, Outer Isles Thrust; MB, Minch Basin; NLB, North Lewis Basin; M, Moho; D, Diffractions due to apparent offset of Moho. (c) The same section after migration and geological modelling, i.e. presented as a distance–depth section. Note that the OIT, in its true position, is responsible for offsetting the Moho. Velocity structure of the model is given in units of km s^{-1}.

Isles Thrust and the Moho! Comparing Figures 3.33b and c, we see how the fault has been steepened, so that, in reality, it intersects and actually displaces the Moho by about 2–3 km. We know from outcrop and from other sections in Figure 3.26 that the Outer Isles Thrust reaches the surface, and we see here how it penetrates the entire crust, cutting the Moho.

What type of stress regime would cause the Moho offset?

Downfaulting has occurred on the upper surface: this is normal fault movement produced by an extensional stress regime. So the Moho offset must be associated with the late, probably Mesozoic, reactivation phase of the thrust fault. This is an important result, because it demonstrates that *localized failure* extended right through the crust during this extensional event and so has interesting rheological implications (Section 3.2.5).

At a deeper level in Figure 3.33, we see another major reflector, this time within the mantle—the so-called **Flannan Thrust**, which penetrates to 14 s TWT, or *c.* 50 km depth. On the geological model (Figure 3.33c), this feature dips at 33° and penetrates the Moho at the eastern end of the WINCH AB section. This penetration is even more obvious on WINCH BC, MOIST and DRUM (Figure 3.26), where the Flannan Thrust can be seen to arise within the lower crust. Before the advent of reflection seismology in Britain, no such deep features had ever been seen, and, indeed, they were quite unexpected, since the upper mantle is normally thought to be ductile under stress and not prone to shearing or faulting (cf. Block 1A, Section 2.2.2). There is no outcropping equivalent of this feature, so we cannot say whether it is, indeed, a thrust. Its dip, reflective character, and the fact that it cuts the Moho have been used to suggest that the Flannan Thrust is some kind of fault that has sheared the rocks in a normally quite ductile region—known as a *shear zone*. In other words, it is a region of localized strain, which may result from the Caledonian orogeny or the period of Mesozoic extension, or it may be another Caledonian thrust reactivated during Mesozoic extension. Indeed, shear zones tend to act as foci for hydrothermal fluid flow, which in the case of the Flannan Thrust, may have produced serpentinized peridotite with a strongly contrasting acoustic impedance.

The DRUM seismic profile was acquired partly to find out how deeply the Flannan Thrust penetrates into the mantle, and Figure 3.26f shows that it is positively identified down to nearly 30 s TWT.

What depth do you estimate for this travel time?

The Moho is at *c.* 9 s, giving 27 km, to which we add a further 21 s at mantle velocities, giving 84 km more, approximately 110 km in all. So the Flannan Thrust cuts through a significant part of the lithosphere, and this has been used to speculate that it could even be the site of an ancient (i.e. pre-Caledonian) subduction zone. If so, it would perhaps have been subject to later shearing movements, hydration and the development of a strong reflection coefficient, when compared with the acoustic properties of mantle peridotite.

Even more unexpected than the Flannan Thrust were the series of strong, almost horizontal reflections, called the *W reflector*, found on the DRUM profile (Figure 3.26f at 13–15 s TWT (45–50 km depth)). This runs continuously over about 100 km of the section, and merges with the Flannan Thrust to the west. Any interpretation of this feature is likely to be even more speculative than that of the Flannan Thrust, but the most likely source is considered to be a sub-horizontal shear zone.

Now that we have introduced many of the more prominent features to be found in the BIRPS reflection seismic profiles, albeit those of northern Scotland, this would be the ideal time to view the final 20 minutes of the video programme accompanying this part of Block 1: *Fragments of Britain*, on video-cassette VC271. The programme continues (after the 20 minute point on the clock) with David Smythe, who looks at the results of the MOIST profile and then discusses the reflection seismic method and its interpretation. (Award yourself a bonus if you spot where the narrator uses the term 'rays' when 'waves' are being described). In describing the manipulation of reflection data to produce true positions, Dave Smythe undertakes both migration and modelling in one step, but you should understand from the preceding text that there are two separate processes involved. This part of the programme should help you to consolidate your understanding of Sections 3.2.1 and 3.2.2.

The final 10 minutes of the programme (30 to 40 on the clock) introduce the seismic reflection data relevant to the Iapetus Suture. Simon Klemperer of the BIRPS group at Cambridge discusses the results from the WINCH EF line that crosses the suture to the west of mainland UK, and then takes a look at the exciting results from the NEC profile run to the east in the North Sea. You have a reduced scale version of the NEC profile, which we shall be discussing together with the accretion and suturing model developed by the BIRPS in the next Section. So don't worry if you find some of the details elusive, as you will soon have the opportunity of studying them more slowly.

Now view the last 20 minutes of *Fragments of Britain*.

3.2.3 Seismic signature of the Iapetus Suture Zone

The identification of the north-dipping Iapetus Suture beneath the Solway Basin between Scotland and Ireland, and beneath the North Sea off the Northumberland coast has proved to be one of the most spectacular results of the BIRPS programme. In this Section, we shall follow the theme of the video programme, first considering the suture line as located on seismic sections, and then exploring the seismic reflection contrasts of the surrounding regions which provide clues about the processes operating during closure of the Iapetus Ocean.

Figure 3.34 is an unmigrated line drawing of the WINCH section EF (cf. Figure 3.26b). Note that for comparison with the NEC profile it is oriented in the opposite direction to the earlier WINCH sections you examined, with north to the left (i.e. as viewed from the west). The suture is marked by the pronounced change in reflection character along a north-dipping boundary between about 10 km depth and the Moho at 30 km depth (*c.* 4–10 s TWT). To the north of this boundary, few reflectors are detected throughout the depth extent of the crust, whereas, to the south, both the middle and lower crust are highly reflective.

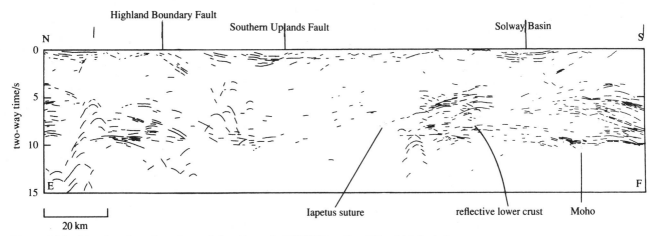

Figure 3.34 Line drawing of unmigrated data from the WINCH section EF, which includes reflections from the Iapetus Suture Zone. Note that north (point E) is at the left of this section.

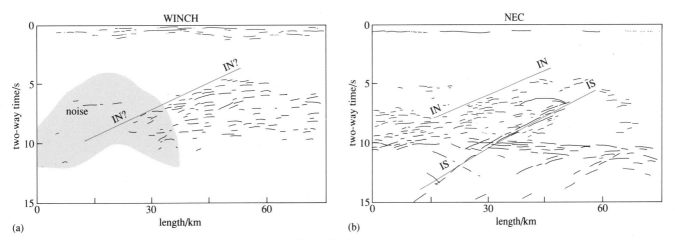

Figure 3.35 Unmigrated line drawings showing the detail of reflections across the Iapetus Suture Zone as seen on the WINCH (a) and NEC (b) profiles. North is at the left on both sections. For discussion of IN and IS, see text.

Nevertheless, this evidence for the location and extent of the Iapetus Suture is limited and inconclusive. Why is this?

(The reasons were discussed in the video programme.)

The definition of the suture on WINCH is limited firstly by noise in the data, which prevents the suture from being traced to or through the Moho. Secondly, the evidence is inconclusive because we have only one profile. Corroboration is required from other sources to prove that the feature is real and not an artefact of sideswipe or data processing.

Figure 3.35 gives detailed line diagrams of the suture area itself as seen on both the WINCH and NEC profiles. In contrast to WINCH, the NEC profile proved to be relatively free of noise, and so features of the Iapetus Suture were defined more clearly. Two prominent north-dipping boundaries occur, 25 km apart in north–south distance, across which there are reflectivity contrasts; these are labelled IS and IN in Figure 3.35b.

What are the reflectivity characteristics of the lower crust to either side of each of these boundaries?

The lower crust is non-reflective to the north of IN, reflective between IN and IS, and is relatively non-reflective again to the south of IS. Not surprisingly, it seems that the Iapetus Suture is a much more complicated zone than revealed by WINCH. In terms of reflectivity contrast, the boundary IN, with non-reflective lower crust to the north, seems more likely to correlate with the single prominent boundary on WINCH—hence the label IN in Figure 3.35a.

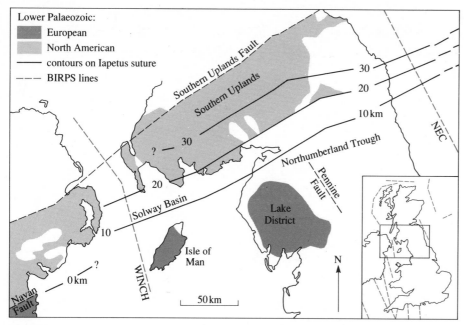

Figure 3.36 Contours on the dipping Iapetus Suture based on a combination of the WINCH and NEC reflection seismic profiles (*cf.* Figure 3.35) and geo-electrical evidence (not discussed in this Block) for deep structure beneath the suture zone. Also indicated are the affinities of the Lower Palaeozoic sedimentary rock types in this area. The Navan fault of eastern Ireland may be a surface expression of the Iapetus Suture, based on faunal and sedimentological criteria.

An attempt has been made to correlate the position of the Iapetus Suture along the strike direction by Simon Klemperer and Drummond Matthews of the BIRPS group—see Figure 3.36, which includes geo-electrical evidence for a highly conductive dipping layer, thought to be the Iapetus Suture, beneath the Northumberland Trough and Southern Uplands of Scotland. Note from Figure 3.35 that more confidence can be placed on the deep position of the suture than on its shallow structure. For example, if the reflectivity boundary on WINCH is projected up-dip, it cuts the surface within the Lower Palaeozoic rocks of the Isle of Man and Lake District. These rocks all have distinct European faunal assemblages, and so there is a problem, because rocks to the northwest of the suture should have North American affinities. Resolution of this discrepancy is possible in a number of ways: (i) the reflectivity boundary may be a crustal feature within the European crust rather than the true position of the suture, (ii) the Iapetus Suture may steepen upwards in the crust, so reaching the surface further north but without a seismic expression, or (iii) the Lower Palaeozoic of the Isle of Man and the Lake District may have been pushed northwards over the deep position of the suture during continental collison. While we do not have the evidence to exclude any one of these possibilities, as you will see below, overthrusting (i.e. item iii) seems to be the most likely.

This brings us to the point where we need to examine and consider the interpretation of the NEC profile in greater detail, so you should now study the folded version of this profile provided.

ITQ 3.8 Start by comparing the unmigrated and migrated sections.

(a) Can you account for the south-dipping diffractions apparently in the upper mantle around SP 1500–1700 on the unmigrated section, i.e. around 65–85 km from the northern end?

(b) Locate the IS boundary on the unmigrated section, which occurs 120 km along the section at 10 s TWT. What happens to this boundary after migration?

(c) What is the approximate Moho depth on the NEC profile, and how variable is this.

(d) Are there any places on the NEC profile where the Moho does not produce a strong reflection?

Before you go any further, you should mark in pencil on the migrated NEC section provided:

(i)   the Moho, continuing this to the southern end of the section at the base of the lower crustal reflective layer;

(ii)   the top of the lower crustal reflective layer between 50 and 120 km and between 180 and 240 km along the section;

(iii)   the most significant reflectors and boundaries between zones of differing reflectivity. IS should be obvious; IN dips from 4 s TWT at 140 km to *c*. 7 s TWT at 120 km. You should also mark a pair of parallel north-dipping reflectors along which the Moho deepens at *c*. 80 km along the section. Label the upper reflector P1 and the lower one P2.

When you have done this, you should have a section looking something like Figure 3.37 to which we have added the four zones of differing seismic reflection characteristics that you met in the video programme and which, by now, should be increasingly obvious from your copy of the NEC profile.

Just to make sure you are absolutely clear about these zones, try the following ITQ.

ITQ 3.9   (a)   What is the difference in lower crustal reflectivity between zones A and B?

(b)   What feature forms the southern boundary of zone B?

(c)   Describe the lower crustal and Moho reflectivity contrasts between zones C and D.

Interpretation of the seismic section is inevitably highly speculative, and we must construct an evolutionary picture based on our independent knowledge of terrane assembly, of surface and plausible deep geology across the Iapetus Suture. As you know from the video programme, zones A–D are thought to represent different terranes involved in the suturing event between the palaeo-North American continent to the north (zone A) and the palaeo-European continent to the south (zone D). The detail is given in Figure 3.38.

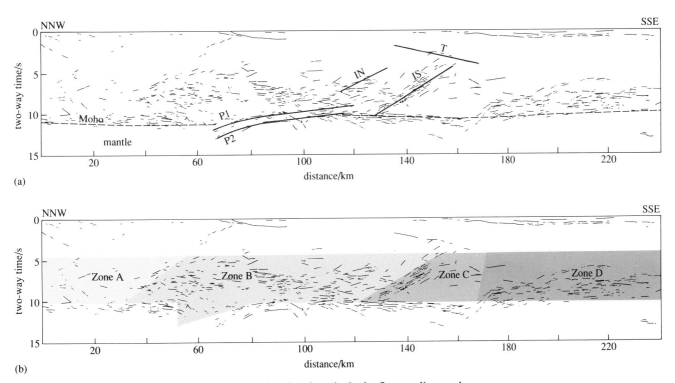

Figure 3.37   Line drawing of migrated NEC data showing the principal reflectors discussed in the text: IS, IN, P1, P2 and the Moho. The significance of reflector T will become clear a little later, in relation to Figures 3.38 and 3.39. Zones A to D are the four terrane fragments assembled during the suturing event.

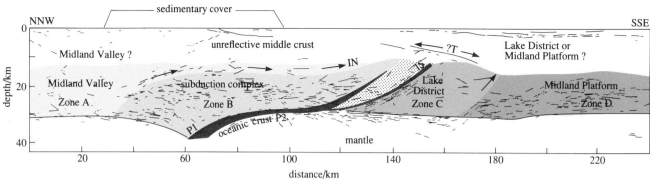

Figure 3.38 Geological interpretation of lower crust on migrated NEC depth section. Arrows indicate probable directions of thrusting during plate closure.

The section starts adjacent to the Midland Valley, but lacks the detailed upper crustal structure revealed by short refraction seismic lines (Section 3.1.3), and gives way southwards to the subduction complex of zone B with its highly reflective lower crust. This area corresponds roughly to the Southern Uplands of Scotland, and the subduction complex is envisaged as including a smeared out prism of Lower Palaeozoic volcaniclastics, with incorporated fragments of the overlying continental crust, originally carried down with the subducted oceanic crust. In this way, the continental foreland of the northern plate would become **underplated** in zone B—see Figure 3.39, which illustrates successive stages in this underplating process.

The continuity of reflectors P1 and P2 on the seismic section suggests that these represent the upper and lower surfaces of an uninterrupted body of rock about 3.5 km thick (*c.* 1 s TWT at a velocity of 7 km s^{-1}). Given that P1 and P2 transect the normal Moho depth to the north and the lower crustal reflectivity to the south, the rock mass responsible was probably *tectonically* emplaced or modified. By analogy with elsewhere in the world, this zone is thought to include imbricated (i.e. tectonically interwoven) sediments and basalts preserved from the subduction event. Quite simply, we are possibly seeing the seismic trace of layers 1 and 2 of the oceanic crust where it has penetrated the continental Moho (see Figure 3.38 between 60 and 100 km along the section). A most important conclusion follows from this analysis of P1 and P2 with the smearing out of the subduction complex. The bottom margin, the present day Moho, *must represent a plane of decoupling* between the crust and mantle. Even after subduction ceased, the decoupled mantle probably continued its northerly motion, thinning and stretching the remnant ocean crust (Figure 3.39d), until, finally, plate motion ceased due to increased friction along the plane of decoupling.

The reflector IN represents, on this model, the top of the subduction complex with IS at its base. But the prominence of the reflections from IS, indicating a high reflection coefficient compared with the rocks above, suggests that IS itself may be a thin flake of high velocity and/or density material. Again it may be a remnant of strongly deformed oceanic crust caught within the suture zone. Its northerly dip again implies that subduction ceased with continental crust of the southern Iapetus margin underthrusting the northern margin.

Immediately south of IS the entire thickness of the crust within the less reflective Lake District zone C is thought to be of volcano-sedimentary arc type, similar to parts of the subduction complex in zone B, but rather less deformed. Zone D probably represents pre-Caledonian basement of the Midlands Craton overlain by Caledonian and younger 'platform' sediments. The basement ridges deduced from potential field evidence (Section 2.3.1) do not have any obvious signature on this seismic section, which terminates off the coast of north Yorkshire.

On the model described above, where would you place the Iapetus suture?

The best-fit position is at IS, which, therefore, is the most fundamental boundary between the northern and southern continents, even though there are minor terrane fragments on either side of this boundary—in zones B and C. Note that this position is a little further south than indicated by Figure 3.36, which was based on the probable correlation of IN on WINCH and with IS on NEC. Finally, what about processes in the upper crust, especially in the suture zone itself?

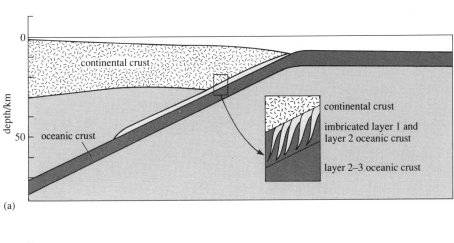

(a)

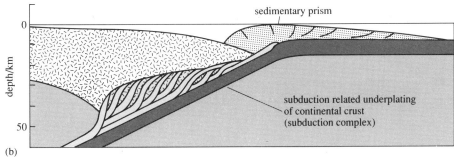

(b)

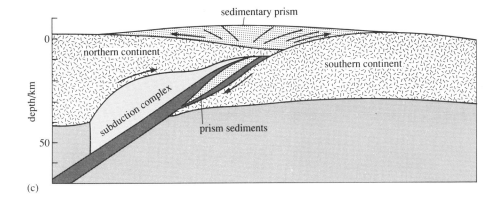

(c)

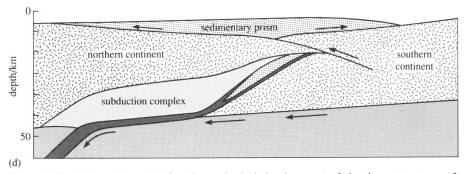

(d)

Figure 3.39 Schematic model for the geological development of the deep structures of northern England and the Iapetus Suture Zone based on the interpretation in Figure 3.38. (a) Early subduction history prior to development of the sedimentary prism but during imbrication of the upper layers of ocean crust. (b) Sedimentary prism now well established; imbrication of ocean crust with slices flaked off overriding continental crust. (c) Initial stages of collision and continental subduction; underthrusting of oceanic crust and lateral transport of sedimentary prism at surface. (d) Subduction complex smeared out beneath northern plate and complex interthrusting between continents in mid-upper crust.

This takes us back to Figure 3.39, where, in stage (a), Iapetus Ocean crust was being subducted beneath the northern continent. In time, the thickness of the oceanic crust in the narrowing ocean was increased as ocean floor volcanics and sediments became deformed and imbricated. As the system developed, with the subduction complex forming at a deep level (Figure 3.39b), a sedimentary prism became established at the surface. During the collision process, underthrusting of the southern continent at depth caused the sedimentary prism to become decoupled and to move laterally across the entire suture zone, especially to the north, as shown in Figures 3.39c and d. Within the fine structure of Figure 3.39d, there is the suggestion that at mid-crustal levels the northern continent was overthrust as well as underthrust by material from the south. This interpretation is based on the reflectivity contrast seen on the migrated seismic section between 140 and 180 km in the upper crust. (This reflectivity boundary is labelled T in Figures 3.37 and 3.38). So, as we anticipated earlier in this Section, it is highly likely that the youngest pre-closure Lower Palaeozoic rocks, forming a sedimentary prism, have been smeared out over the suture zone itself. Moreover, during the final stages of closure, *some of the arc-related crust of zone C*, in the Lake District and Isle of Man, *may well have been carried north*, perhaps by tens of kilometres, from their true original position.

Although speculative, especially towards the end, we hope you will agree that our examination of the NEC profile has been extremely revealing in terms of lithosphere convergence processes. And what of the Iapetus Suture itself? It appears that this major north-dipping tectonic break has been identified in the middle and lower crust beneath northernmost England and southern Scotland. If it reached the surface, it would probably cut through the central Lake District, rather further south than originally envisaged (e.g. Block 1, Figure 3.27), and even a shade further south than indicated in Figure 3.36!

3.2.4 Seismic signature of the Variscan terrane

Our final set of seismic sections comes from the southwest approaches of Britain—the SWAT lines (Figure 3.25). These are located in the region affected by Variscan tectonics and cross the expected position of the Variscan Front (cf. Block 1A, Figures 3.21–3.23 and Block 1B, Figures 2.14 and 2.15). In particular, SWAT lines 2 and 4 (Figure 3.40) provide excellent images of the Front, which acts as quite a

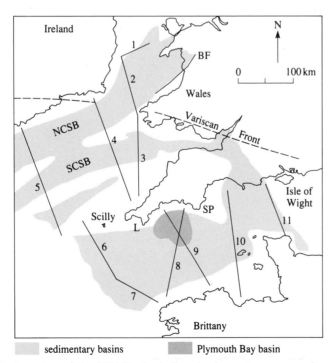

Figure 3.40 Location of the SWAT seismic lines in the western approaches and English Channel. Sedimentary basins are pale pink and the deep Plymouth Bay Basin is darker pink. Numbers refer to profiles, some of which are shown in Figure 3.41 and are discussed in the text. NCSB, North Celtic Sea Basin; SCSB, South Celtic Sea Basin; L, Lizard; SP, Start Point; BF, Bala Fault System.

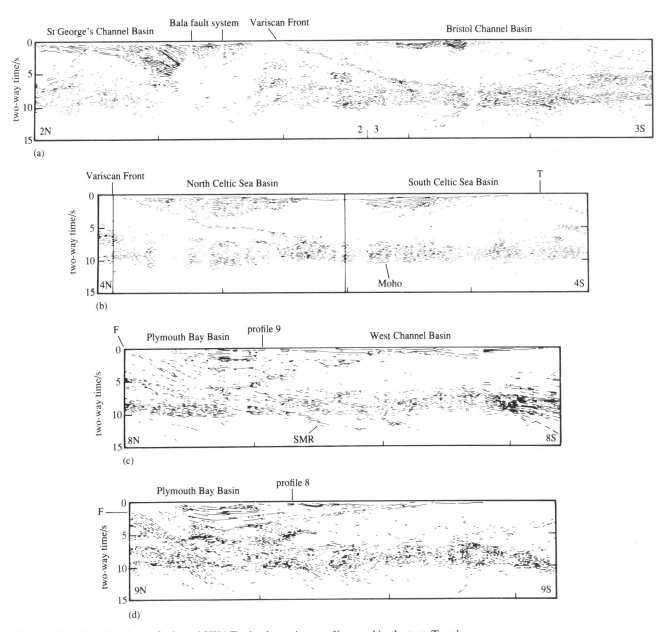

Figure 3.41 Line drawings of selected SWAT seismic sections as discussed in the text. T and F are possible thrusts, and SMR is a sub-Moho reflection. (The ticks on the horizontal scales are 50 km apart.)

strong south-dipping reflector traversing the upper crust and merging with highly reflective lower crust at *c.* 7 s TWT (Figure 3.41a and b). The Variscan Front is a much more flat-lying structure than the Iapetus Suture, with a *mean* apparent dip in these unmigrated sections of 17° (approaching 19° after migration). This supports the 'thin skinned' view of Variscan tectonics developed in Section 2.3.1 from potential field data and illustrated in Figure 2.15. In particular, the dip of the front is quite variable, as seen on SWAT line 4.

How does dip vary along the length (i.e. down-dip) of the front in this seismic profile?

The dip is steeper in the crust, along the first *c.* 40 km of section, but then flattens out to nearly horizontal at 5 s TWT. A change in depth of 15 km along 40 km of section gives a dip of 21°. Such steeper parts of thrust faults are sometimes known as 'ramps' with 'flats' between; overall this type of geometry is often termed **ramp and flat geometry**. Correlation with other commercial seismic data gives a strike for this fault of 100°, similar to the local strike of the Variscan Front on-shore as depicted in Figure 3.40 and elsewhere.

Now examine the upper crust above and behind the Variscan Front on the two seismic sections (Figures 3.41a and b). What is the most important feature of this zone?

In this area are sedimentary basins, the shallow Bristol Channel Basin on lines 2–3, and the deeper North Celtic Sea Basin on line 4, extending nearly to 4 s TWT. Thus, as with the BIRPS profiles off northern Scotland, we have post-tectonic younger sedimentary basins which may have developed and filled during reactivation as the hanging wall rotated downwards (Figure 3.27). As you know from the potential field data (Section 2.3.3), the North Celtic Sea Basin is one of the deepest Mesozoic–Tertiary basins around coastal Britain. In fact, it is filled with Triassic to late Cretaceous sedimentary rocks down to about 9 km (based on a P-wave velocity of $4.5 \, \text{km s}^{-1}$).

Several other south-dipping reflectors were recognized on the SWAT sections. For example, reflector T in Figure 3.41b has a slightly steeper dip than the Variscan Front, but has been traced with on-shore reflection profiling east of the Cornubian batholith and has a Variscan strike. Thus it is probably also a Variscan thrust. Further south, reflection profiles across the English Channel (lines 8 and 9 in Figure 3.40, see Figure 3.41c and d) show some steeply dipping reflections, labelled F, which cross the entire crust and the Moho (cf. the Outer Isles Thrust of northern Scotland). After migration, however, these F reflectors are found to lie entirely within the crust, above the Moho.

Looking at the position of profiles 8 and 9 in Figure 3.40, what geological structure is likely to be responsible for the reflector F?

This is probably the thrust that carried the Lizard ophiolite into position—often known as the Lizard-Start Thrust since Lizard-like schists and gneisses also occur as a thin coastal sliver at Start Point (GR275035).

Once again a Mesozoic–Tertiary sedimentary basin—the *Plymouth Bay Basin* (see Figure 3.40)—is superimposed at shallow levels above the dipping thrust. You will recall from Section 2.3.1 that there is a prominent gravity ridge extending east from Cornwall and immediately south of the Lizard–Start thrust, implying that relatively dense rocks overlie the thrust across this area. It is perhaps surprising, then, that crustal reflectivity does not change markedly across reflector F (Figures 3.41c and d). Moreover, the positive gravity anomalies across this area occur despite the existence of low-density rocks of the Plymouth Bay Basin. We must infer that high-density rocks occupy significant parts of the middle and lower crust across this area. Here it is perhaps significant that the dipping reflectors in SWAT profiles 8 and 9 extend into the mantle, suggesting that basic–ultrabasic (ophiolitic) rock slivers may have been transported upwards by the thrust from these deep root zones. Otherwise, the reflectivity pattern of the Variscan terrane is very similar to that of the Caledonian crust further north, with a generally seismically transparent upper crust, a highly reflective lower crust, and a mantle at 10 s TWT. In summary, a clear picture of the two main Variscan thrusts discussed in earlier sections has been produced by reflection seismology: the Variscan Front is a shallow-dipping ramp and flat thrust, which, at its base, merges with a reflective lower crust, whereas the Lizard–Start Thrust is a rather more steeply dipping structure, which has its roots at the base of the crust, or possibly in the upper mantle.

3.2.5 Seismic evidence for lithosphere rheology

In this final Section of Block 1, we come full circle by returning to the theme of Block 1A, Section 2.2, to examine the implications of the seismic data we have now introduced for the physical characteristics of the lithosphere. A full discussion of this subject appears in Block 5, so the objective here is simply to build bridges between these different parts of Block 1 and then give a few forward pointers. Some of the most relevant features of the BIRPS seismic sections are:

1   Reflections from low-angle upper crustal thrust faults often merge with or are lost in the reflective layer of the lower crust (e.g. the Moine Thrust, the Variscan Front), whereas others penetrate through this layer to the upper mantle (e.g. the

Outer Isles Thrust and, possibly, the Lizard–Start Thrust). The reflections from the more prominent upper mantle features, such as the Flannan Thrust, seem to terminate in the lower crust.

2   The lower crust has a highly reflective nature comprising numerous short sub-horizontal reflections (e.g. Figure 3.28).

3   The depth to the Moho is quite constant throughout Britain, despite the massive crustal thickening effects of the Caledonian and Variscan orogenies.

> Can you recall from Block 1A, Section 2.2, where the lithosphere, and particularly the crust, is most likely to undergo (a) brittle fracture and (b) ductile flow when subject to tectonic stress?

The upper crust always has a brittle fracture zone (the thickness of which depends on heat flow, accumulated stress and time—Block 1A, Figure 2.20) whereas the lower crust and mantle lithosphere are generally more ductile (cf. Block 1A, Figure 2.23 and related discussion). At first sight, therefore, it is perhaps difficult to understand why seemingly localized fractures cross ductile regions in the lower crust and upper mantle. Clearly, we would expect brittle faulting in the cool upper crust, but why apparently at greater depths? The answer is that we are probably not seeing evidence of brittle faulting, but rather, within ductile layers, deformation which is confined to *shear zones* within which there is a network of creep dislocations (Figure 3.42). Such shear zones, it is argued, would be narrow enough that they might be indistinguishable on seismic sections from much sharper brittle fault zones.

A shearing (or strain-banding) model has also been put forward for the origin of lower crustal reflectivity (see relevant parts of Section 3.2.2), but this model is by no means unique. For example, injection of basic sills, or layered igneous intrusions into the lower crust and the presence of open, fluid-filled cracks have all been suggested as possible explanations of this layering. It has been noted that the depth to the top of the lower crustal reflective layer can be correlated with the magnitude of surface heat flow, suggesting that a temperature-dependent rheological phenomenon may provide a possible explanation.

Unfortunately, there are difficulties with all of these models. For example, there is a question of exactly why shear zones should be strongly reflective, of whether basic sill generation could be sufficiently voluminous to produce reflective lower crust over such wide areas, and of whether the lower crust is sufficiently impermeable to retain trapped fluids over long time-scales. Similarly, if reflectivity in the lower crust is a product of *former* tectonic activity, it seems strange that the depth of the reflective zone is so well correlated with *present-day* heat flow. Today, despite the objections, increasing weight is being placed on the importance of basic magmatism during extension of the lithosphere which may produce layered intrusions in the lower crust. However, we return to this debate in Block 5.

The final feature on which a comment is necessary concerns the similarity of Moho depth throughout Britain. We know that young mountain belts such as the Alps, Himalayas and Andes have a thickened crust (70–80 km in places), so why do we

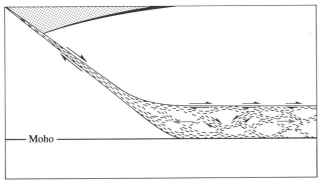

Figure 3.42 Deformation in the lower crust probably involves a shear zone network involving many small-scale sub-zones in which creep displacements occur.

not have similarly thick crust beneath the Caledonides and the Variscan areas of Britain?

Can you suggest at least one reason?

Erosion will have removed material from the surface, of course, which acts to reduce crustal thickness, but lateral flow of ductile material in the lower crust and mantle may also provide a mechanism for smoothing the base of the crust. You may remember encountering this isostatic readjustment process before at the end of Block 1A, Section 2.2.3; it is illustrated in Block 1A, Figure 2.33, to which you should refer as a reminder. Now we have seismic reflection data that are consistent with the operation of this mass movement process near the crust–mantle boundary. Moreover, we have hypothesized from the NEC seismic section, just north of the Iapetus Suture, that crust–mantle decoupling occurred during tectonic thrusting. This should strike a warning bell for you, however, because on the one hand we are arguing for reducing crustal thickness by lateral ductile flow of material within and beneath the crust, while on the other, we need features produced during mountain-building processes to survive intact for 400 Ma. Clearly, the evolution of Moho topography is a complex process, requiring flow not simply at the crust–mantle boundary but in some adjacent regions of the ductile lowermost crust and deeper ductile mantle. Perhaps the uppermost mantle, like the upper crust, is resistant to flow, as we might expect on rheological grounds (due to the olivine-rich mineralogy), so that the decay of crustal thickness is principally a lower crustal process. Again we will return to consider this process more fully in Block 5.

That completes our survey of the geophysical evidence for the structure and behaviour of the UK lithosphere. Subsequent Blocks examine modern tectonic processes at different types of plate boundary and include a detailed look at past tectonism as represented in the UK. We hope you will find this broad framework useful in your study of the remainder of this Course.

Summary

1   In Section 3.2, we have dealt with seismic reflection techniques and their use in determining lithosphere structure, with particular reference to Britain. We started by showing how separate seismic traces with prominent reflections can be displayed side by side in order to construct a seismic section (Figure 3.14) in which distance is plotted horizontally against two-way time. By shading strong arrivals from each prominent reflection, we obtain dark and bright lines across the section. These represent reflection continuity, and so define reflectors where the value of reflection coefficient (equation 3.6) is high because of the strong contrast in acoustic impedance (equation 3.5) of the adjacent rocks.

2   We then examined the construction of seismic sections in more detail, which is carried out using multi-channel reflection surveying (Figure 3.19). Several traces are collected from around a common mid-point, and are adjusted for zero offset time using the normal move-out correction so that they can be stacked to improve the quality of the signal, reduce noise, etc. (Figure 3.21). Problems arise, however, when reflectors are not horizontal because their apparent dip is then less than their true dip on seismic sections (Figure 3.23 and equation 3.7); the process of migration places all reflectors in their correct space–time position. Migration also removes the diffraction hyperbolae that may be seen in raw (unmigrated) sections and are caused by the scattering of seismic energy at terminations of sharp curves on an interface.

3   The conversion of a seismic section into a true depth section requires a knowledge of the seismic propagation velocities of the different geological layers involved. In seismic modelling, ray tracing techniques are used and even entire synthetic seismic sections (e.g. Figure 3.24) may be constructed from best estimates of the geological/velocity structure. These can be compared with the original seismic section, which can then be modified accordingly.

4   We then examined a number of the BIRPS seismic reflection profiles from UK off-shore areas (Figure 3.25), many of which were presented as line drawings for

simplicity. A good rule of thumb is that with typical crust and mantle velocities of 6 and 8 km s^{-1} we need to multiply TWT by 3 and 4 respectively to obtain approximate depths. A review of the MOIST, WINCH and DRUM lines off northern Scotland, the NEC line off northeast England, and the SWAT lines off southwest England revealed the following principal features:

(a)   In the uppermost crust, we find some prominent shallow sedimentary basins that have a seismically layered structure and resemble half-grabens, produced on rotational normal faults, which in some cases are due to the reactivation of older dipping thrusts beneath (Figure 3.27).

(b)   Otherwise the upper crust down to $c.$ 4–5 s TWT is commonly seismically transparent in the UK.

(c)   In some parts of Britain, there are short, sub-horizontal reflections from the middle crust (4–6 s TWT) but the lower crust (6–10 s TWT) is strongly reflective almost everywhere (Figure 3.28).

(d)   The Moho is at an almost constant travel time around Britian (9–10 s TWT), though there is evidence from the migrated WINCH profile (Figure 3.33) and from the NEC profile (Figure 3.37) that displacements both across and along the Moho have occurred during tectonic thrusting.

(e)   The mantle lithosphere imaged by the BIRPS lines is also seismically transparent apart from some major deep reflectors that represent thrusts or shear zones (see f below).

(f)   The Moine Thrust, the Great Glen Fault and the Variscan Front produce prominent reflections that traverse the upper crust but merge downwards with the lower crustal reflective layer; the Outer Isles Thrust and the Lizard–Start Thrust penetrate down to the upper mantle; the Flannan Thrust and the W reflector (on the DRUM line) are prominent in the mantle (e.g. Figure 3.26f) and merge upwards with the lower crustal reflective layer.

(5)   The rheological interpretation of some of these features may be summarized as follows:

(a)   The pentration of apparently localized fault/thrust structures across almost the entire lithosphere at first sight seems inconsistent with the presence of ductile regions in the lower crust and upper mantle. However, it is likely that such structures may be able to cross ductile layers in the form of broad shear zones where there is a network of creep dislocations. Moreover, at least some of the trans-lithosphere reflectors represent previous plate boundaries.

(b)   Lower crustal reflectivity may also result from the operation of strong horizontal shearing stresses producing ductile strain banding across this region. Alternative possibilities are that fluid-filled microfracture networks may occur in the lower crust that are resistant to destruction within a ductile layer, or that basic sills/layered igneous complexes are common in the lower crust.

(c)   The near-constant depth to the Moho across regions of former tectonism suggests that isostatically driven lateral flow of material, probably within the ductile lower crust, has smoothed the topography of this crust–mantle boundary.

6   In a detailed examination of the WINCH and particularly the NEC profile off the coasts of northern England and southern Scotland, the position and strike of the north-dipping ($c.$ 30°) Iapetus Suture has been located (see Figure 3.36). A detailed geological interpretation of the NEC profile indicates that between the palaeo-North American continent to the north and the palaeo-European continent to the south are (Figure 3.38) a subduction complex and a volcano-sedimentary arc. At the surface, these correspond roughly to the Southern Uplands and Lake District areas. At depth, the subduction complex is smeared out even to the extent of displacing the Moho, and has thus underplated the continental foreland north of the suture. In this interpretation, the reflectors IN and IS in Figure 3.38 represent, respectively, the top and bottom of the subduction complex. IS is the most fundamental boundary between the northern and southern Caledonian plates and is the favoured position of the Iapetus Suture; if back-projected, it would cut the surface in the central Lake

District. However, it does not reach the surface, probably because it has been overthrust by arc complex rocks from the south.

7 Reflection seismic data on the Variscan Front confirm that it is a shallow-dipping (c. 19° average) ramp and flat thrust structure which strikes at about 100° across southern Britain. Behind the Front and overlapping the Variscan terrane south of the Cornubian peninsula is the Lizard–Start Thrust, which carries ophiolitic rocks possibly from a mantle root zone to the south where the reflector terminates. The overall seismic characteristics of the British Variscan area are very similar to those of the Caledonides further north (e.g. Figure 3.41).

SAQS FOR SECTION 3

SAQ 3.1 State, with reasons, whether each of the following statements is true or false:

(a) Reflection seismic profiles in off-shore areas around Britain have been generally more successful than refraction experiments for locating the subsurface positions of major fault structures.

(b) After converting from TWT to depth, using correct velocities, dipping structures on seismic reflection profiles appear with their true dip as it would appear on a correct geological section.

(c) Seismic reflection profiles around Britain have shown that some of the Mesozoic sedimentary basins may have formed during extensional reactivation on major dipping thrusts that lie beneath the basins.

(d) Seismic refraction experiments have shown that high-density, high grade metamorphic rocks occur at shallower depths beneath the Midland Valley of Scotland than beneath adjacent regions.

(e) The passage of deep fault structures through the lower crust means that this otherwise ductile layer must be capable of brittle failure.

(f) According to the model presented in Section 3.2.3, the Iapetus Suture does not occur at the surface in mainland UK, having been overthurst by arc-related crust from the south.

SAQ 3.2 In two or three sentences each, explain the significance of the following terms for enhancing the quality of seismic data and their interpretation:

(a) reduced time–distance graphs

(b) normal move-out corrections

(c) seismic modelling.

SAQ 3.3 A low-angle (20° dip) thrust brings ophiolitic rocks across a volcaniclastic arc formed above a former subduction zone. The rocks beneath the thrust are mainly rhyolites and shales while those above are gabbros and peridotites

(a) How well do you think this thrust will be recorded in a seismic section;

(b) What will be the dip of the thrust on an unmigrated section; and

(c) What other prominent feature might be recorded in the vicinity of the thrust prior to migration?

SAQ 3.4 What happens to a seismic wave on reaching an interface across which the rocks have

(a) the same propagation velocity but different density;

(b) the same density but different propagation velocity?

SAQ 3.5 In a sentence each, what is the evidence for each of the following assertions:

(a) The LISPB seismic refraction data include reflected wave arrivals from the Moho.

(b)   Some geological structures responsible for dipping reflectors as recorded by the BIRPS programme may penetrate much of the mantle lithosphere.

(c)   According to the interpretation of NEC presented in this Block, during the late stages of closure of the Iapetus Ocean it is likely that tectonic decoupling occurred with thrusting along the crust–mantle boundary.

(d)   The Lizard–Start Thrust appears to have carried ophiolitic rocks across the area of the present-day Plymouth Bay Basin, which, paradoxically, contains low-density rocks in a region of positive Bouguer gravity.

ITQ ANSWERS AND COMMENTS

ITQ 2.1 The average densities of both sandstone and granite are lower than for gneisses, so both cases would probably generate *negative gravity anomalies*. Of course, the density ranges for all three rock types overlap, but, taking average values, case (a) would produce a stronger gravity anomaly than case (b). Similarly, gneisses are more magnetic than either granite or sandstone, so, at first sight, similar negative magnetic anomalies would be produced by both cases. (The real situation is a good deal more complicated than this as you will find in Section 2.2). It appears that a *seismic* experiment would have the best chance of distinguishing between the two, for wave velocities in sandstone are generally lower and have a much wider range than for granite and gneiss which have identical ranges of wave velocity. Thus situation (a) would be much more obvious seismically than situation (b).

ITQ 2.2 (a) The difference is $9.832 - 9.780 = 0.052 \text{ m s}^{-2}$. Now $1 \text{ mGal} = 10^{-5} \text{ m s}^{-2}$, so 0.052 m s^{-2} is $5\,200$ mGal.

(b) Typical anomalies are $100-1\,000 \times 10^{-6} \text{ m s}^{-2}$, or $10-100$ mGal, which is between 50 and 500 times smaller than the pole to equator gravity difference.

(c) Gravimeters measure down to 1 part in 10^8 of the Earth's gravity field, which is $c.\ 1 \times 10^{-7} \text{ m s}^{-2}$, or 0.01 mGal; they are between $1\,000$ and $10\,000$ times more sensitive than the size of a typical anomaly.

ITQ 2.3 A reasonable value for the regional field is $+10$ mGal. The Bouguer gravity values at the centres of the anomalies are:

A, -8 mGal; B, -14 mGal; C, 0 mGal.

Thus the residual anomalies due to the granite masses alone are:

A, -18 mGal; B, -24 mGal; C, -10 mGal.

ITQ 2.4 See completed Table 2.3 (Table A1) for answers.

ITQ 2.5 See completed Table 2.4 (Table A2) for answers.

ITQ 2.6 Equation 2.4 states: $\Delta g = 2\pi\, G \Delta \rho t \times 10^5$ mGal.

In this case: $60 = 2\pi\, 6.67 \times 10^{-11} \times 0.1 \times 10^3 \times t \times 10^5$,

whence $t = 14\,317$, or 14.3 km.

ITQ 3.1 Substituting in equation 3.2, which states:

$$h = \frac{x_d}{2} \sqrt{\frac{v_2 - v_1}{v_2 + v_1}}, \text{ we have } 35 = \frac{x_d}{2} \sqrt{\frac{1.5}{14.5}} = \frac{x_d}{2} \times 0.322$$

So $x_d = \dfrac{35 \times 2}{0.322} = 217$ km

So we would need a refraction line at least 217 km long to be sure of obtaining first arrivals from the Moho.

ITQ 3.2 The direct wave, with the lower velocity, has the shallower gradient $= -0.27/100 = -0.0027$.

From equation 3.4, $-0.0027 = 1/v_1 - 1/6 = 1/v_1 - 0.1667$.

So $1/v_1 = 0.164$, whence v_1 (direct wave) $= 6.1 \text{ km s}^{-1}$.

For the refracted wave, extrapolated to the reduced travel time axis, we have a gradient of $-2.56/200 = -0.0128$

Table A1 Potential field characteristics in Britain (answer to ITQ 2.4)

Tectonic trend	Features	Orientation	Gravity expression	Magnetic expression
(a) Hebridean Craton	gneisses of Outer Isles and NW Scotland	NE–SW	(a) Gravity highs with steep gradients to east of Outer Isles	Strong NW–SE anomalies, especially over NW Scotland
(b) Northern Caledonides	Great Glen Fault	NE–SW	(b) Steep gradients (gravity decreasing SE), especially at west end of Moray Firth	40 km wide zone of positive anomalies along fault
	Highland Boundary Fault	NE–SW	Steep gradient, gravity increasing to SE	Steep gradients, field strength increasing SE, and linear anomalies
	Southern Uplands Fault	NE–SW	Gentle gravity gradient, gravity decreasing SE	Narrow linear zone of positive anomalies
(c) Southern Caledonides	Church Stretton Fault Zone	NE–SW	(c) Variable gradient, gravity generally decreasing SE	Series of linear magnetic anomalies
	margins of North Celtic Sea Basin	NE–SW	Steep gradients defining low within basin	Little effect
	Malvern Fault	N–S	Steep gradients, gravity decreasing east into the Worcestershire Basin	Linear positive anomalies
	E England Tornquist Trend and Pennine Fault System	NW–SE	Series of broad linear gravity highs, steep gradients at the Pennine Fault System	Positive magnetic ridges with sharp gradients. Pennine Fault System has little effect
(d) Variscan Orogenic Belt	Variscan Front and trends in S/SW England	W–E	(d) No distinct single feature, but W–E linear zones of moderate/steep gradient on relief map	Little expression, but magnetic highs to north mark edge of Variscan Front in S Wales and SE England
(e) Tertiary Igneous Province	trends formed by igneous centres and Tertiary dykes	NW–SE	(e) Strong positive anomalies over igneous centres, otherwise little effect	Marked NNW–SSE to NW–SE linear anomalies parallel to dyke trend (see also Plate 1.2)

From equation 3.4, $-0.0128 = 1/v_2 - 1/6 = 1/v_2 - 0.1667$

So $1/v_2 = 0.154$, whence v_2 (refracted wave) $= 6.5$ km s^{-1}

From the graph, we see that $x_d = 90$ km, so applying equation 3.2:

$$h = \frac{x_d}{2}\sqrt{\frac{v_2 - v_1}{v_2 + v_1}} = \frac{90}{2}\sqrt{\frac{6.5 - 6.1}{6.5 + 6.1}} = 45\sqrt{\frac{0.4}{12.6}} = 8.02 \text{ km}$$

So the thickness of the upper layer is 8 km.

ITQ 3.3 Following the method in ITQ 3.2, the a_1 line gradient is $-0.7/60 = -0.011\,67$, so the velocity is 6.45 km s^{-1}. For the d line, the gradient is $-1.5/40 = -0.0375$ giving a velocity of 7.74 km s^{-1}. (Note that the equation is very sensitive to precise measurement and you may have values differing by up to 0.5 km s^{-1} from ours).

The a_1 velocity is too fast for shallow metasedimentary layers, which have velocities <6.0, and must come from deeper in the crust; the d-layer velocity only falls within the range for peridotite in Table 2.2, so this must be the mantle.

ITQ 3.4 The main differences are in the upper crustal layering and the definition of the lower crust and Moho. LISPB shows a c. 15 km thick a_0 layer (5.6–6.0 km s^{-1}), whereas the CSSP velocities are slightly lower (5.5–5.7 km s^{-1}) and the layer is much thinner at c. 2 km. This difference is compensated by the greater thickness, 13 km, of the 6.15 km s^{-1} layer in CSSP compared with only c. 5 km of 6.3 km s^{-1} material in LISPB. CSSP defines a 6.6 km s^{-1} lower crust, with a lower velocity than beneath the northern Caledonides, and a Moho at 30 km depth, around the UK average according to LISPB.

ITQ 3.5 The locations of these features are shown on Figure A1. Structures that have an anticlinal appearance occur at SP 2170, 1.6–2.5 s, at SP 1870, 1.8–2.65 s and at SP 1530, 3.3 s. There are structures with a synclinal appearance at SP 800, 3.6 s, at SP 1700, 3.5 s, at SP 1950, 2.8 s and a less obvious one at SP 2100, 3.2 s. There are faults which disturb the local reflection continuity at SP 1870, SP 1400, SP 930 and SP 700. These are rather difficult to identify, and you may have found them, and the two unconformities (where reflectors merge on Figure A1) rather difficult to spot.

ITQ 3.6 Using equation 3.6, we have:

(a) Granite $z = 2\,640 \times 5\,750 = 1.518 \times 10^7$ kg m^{-2} s^{-1}

Limestone $z = 2\,550 \times 4\,000 = 1.020 \times 10^7$ kg m^{-2} s^{-1}

Cancelling out the powers of 10, we have:

$$R = \frac{1.518 - 1.020}{1.518 + 1.020} = \frac{0.498}{2.538} = 0.20$$

(b) Rhyolite $z = 2\,520 \times 3\,300 = 8.316 \times 10^6$ kg m^{-2} s^{-1}

Shales $z = 2\,400 \times 2\,850 = 6.840 \times 10^6$ kg m^{-2} s^{-1}

Table A2 Answer to ITQ 2.5 (Note that in these responses, we have said little about the effects of the regional field; award yourself a bonus if you tried to compensate for this more fully)

Tectonic 'age'	Intrusion or complex	Gravity anomaly: pattern and amplitude	Magnetic anomaly: pattern and amplitude
(a) Northern Caledonides	Strath Halladale	(a) No obvious anomaly	Slight magnetic effect
	Cairngorm-Aberdeen	Large negative anomaly coincident with outcrop, 50–60 mGal	Broad positive anomalies, reaching 200 nT over parts of these intrusions
	Aberdeenshire Gabbros	Strong positive anomalies reaching 50 mGal, but smaller and variable over north of outcrop	Very strong positive anomalies, reaching 500 nT, steep gradients over outcrop margins
	Etive–Rannoch Moor	Negative anomalies, peaking at 50 mGal over Etive, where anomaly coincides with outcrop	Variable small width anomalies over outcrop area, reaching 500 nT over west of Etive
(b) Southern Caledonides	Cheviot	(b) Negative anomaly, reaching 20 mGal over centre of intrusion	Positive anomaly, reaching 300 nT over edges of intrusion
	Weardale—Lake District	Negative anomalies, 30 mGal over Weardale, 15 mGal over Lakes (where regional is more positive)	Slightly negative magnetic anomaly, except at Shap (GR355510), where size of stronger anomaly is indistinct
	Wensleydale	15 mGal negative anomaly over centre of buried intrusion	Magnetic high across intrusion, reaching 150 nT over west
	Market Weighton	35 mGal negative anomaly over centre of postulated intrusion, but in area of negative regional	100 nT positive anomaly, sharper than gravity anomaly
(c) Variscan	SW England batholith	(c) 25 mGal negative anomalies over each intrusion, but in area of positive regional, so effect closer to −50 mGal	No obvious anomalies except over northern edge (discussed earlier)
(d) Tertiary	Skye	(d) Concentric 70 mGal positive anomaly, peaking over west of intrusive complex	500 nT positive (east) and negative (west) anomalies over intrusive complex
	Mull	Concentric 60 mGal positive anomaly over central igneous complex	1 000 nT positive anomaly over intrusive complex, surrounded by strong negative anomaly
	Lundy	50 mGal positive anomaly centred 20 km west of island but located in zone of strong positive regional, so effect closer to +15 mGal	Small positive anomaly, reaching 50 nT over island, but located within −50 nT regional

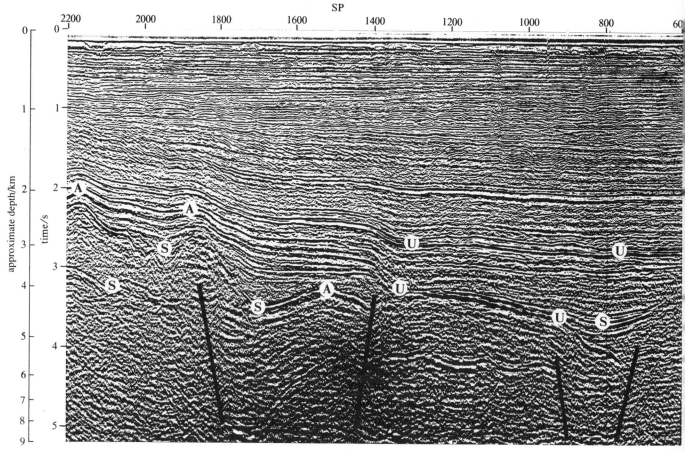

SP

Figure A1 Answer to ITQ 3.5. Structures of anticlinal form are marked by (A) and those of synclinal form by (S), faults by heavy lines, and unconformities by (U).

So $R = \dfrac{8.316 - 6.840}{8.316 + 6.840} = \dfrac{1.476}{15.156} = 0.10$

(c) Granulite $z = 2\,650 \times 6\,250 = 16.56 \times 10^6 \, \text{kg m}^{-2} \, \text{s}^{-1}$

So $R = \dfrac{16.56 - 6.84}{16.56 + 6.84} = \dfrac{9.72}{23.40} = 0.42$

So, case (a) would give a very strong reflection, case (b) a moderate reflection, and case (c) an exceptionally strong reflection. (Note, of course, that we have used mean values for density and velocity; considerable variations occur in nature.)

ITQ 3.7 (i) On most of the sections, there are parallel dipping reflectors in the uppermost crust. These dip to the west at a shallow angle on the MOIST and DRUM profiles; they extend as groups over 10–20 km of section and apparently are terminated against easterly-dipping single reflectors. On the WINCH profile, these parallel groups of dipping reflectors are less obvious, but they still occur, in a more horizontal attitude, where sedimentary basins are marked on the sections.

(ii) The rest of the upper crust down to 4 s TWT contains isolated dipping reflectors, in some cases groups of reflectors as at the eastern end of MOIST, but is otherwise comparatively free of prominent reflections.

ITQ 3.8 (a) It would appear that there are some strong diffraction hyperbolae in this part of the section; most of the south-dipping diffractions disappear after migration, suggesting they are perhaps produced by small diffractors in the lower crust rather than due to real reflectors in the mantle (cf. Figure 3.17).

(b) This boundary steepens from about 25° to nearly 30° dip to the north on migration, and thus its true position is further south (in the up-dip direction—cf. Figures 3.22 and 3.23), as revealed by the migrated section. It also does not extend beneath the Moho.

(c) The Moho occurs at about 10 s TWT across most of the section and thus would be at a depth of *c.* 30 km (slightly greater than on some of the west coast seismic lines considered earlier). There is a very obvious disturbance between 50 and 80 km along the section where the Moho appears to be deeper, at 11–12 s TWT. There are also minor disturbances around 150–170 km along the section, but here the Moho seems to be continuous above some upper mantle reflections.

(d) The strong Moho reflections that occur from 0 to 170 km along the section at *c.* 10 s TWT are lost to the south, though strongly reflective lower crust does occur, particularly at the extreme southern end of the profile.

ITQ 3.9 (a) Lower crustal reflections are much more prominent, continuous and gently curved within zone B; they are present but are more diffuse in zone A, where, incidentally, some reflections also occur in the upper crust.

(b) This is the prominent dipping reflector IS discussed earlier.

(c) Lower crustal reflections in zone C are generally weaker and more diffuse than in zone D, but there is a prominent Moho reflection, which zone D lacks.

SAQ ANSWERS AND COMMENTS

SAQ 2.1 (a) This is the International Gravity Formula, which is used to predict the value of acceleration due to gravity at sea-level over the Earth's surface. It provides a convenient way of finding the value of gravity at a particular latitude in the absence of any zones of anomalous mass, which may therefore be isolated by removing the IGF from observed gravity. (Of course, there are other corrections for height, topography, etc., which must also be made.) (See Section 2.2.1).

(b) This is the International Geomagnetic Reference Field, which, like the IGF, is used to predict the value of the Earth's magnetic field at a particular time and place. Again, after the IGRF has been subtracted from the observed magnetic field strength, the remainder should be due to lithospheric anomalies. (See Section 2.2.1).

(c) This is natural remanent magnetization, which is the permanent magnetism frozen into rocks as they cool through their Curie temperatures. NRM clearly reflects the strength and direction of the geomagnetic field at the time when the rock formed, so can be useful in assessing the latitude at which the magnetism was acquired—vital for palaeomagnetic studies of tectonic plate movements. (See Section 2.2.1).

(d) Regional fields are those due to the sum of all lithospheric potential field anomalies that arise from sources other than that being investigated (e.g. the east–west regional gravity gradient across Britain). The regional field must be assessed and subtracted in order to isolate the anomaly of interest (e.g. Figure 2.7—see also Section 2.2.2).

SAQ 2.2 (c), (e) and (f) are true; (a), (b) and (d) are false.

(a) The increase in gravity over the Equator due to the excess mass is much smaller than the increase of gravity over the poles arising from the poles being much closer to the centre of mass of the Earth (thus r is smaller in the inverse square law of gravitation, equation 2.1, so F is larger at the poles).

(b) Using equation 2.4, the infinite slab approximation, we have $\Delta g = 2\pi G \Delta \rho t \times 10^5$ mGal, so $24 = 2\pi \ 6.67 \times 10^{-11} \times 140 \times t \times 10^5$, whence $t = 4.09$ km. This is a *minimum* thickness, because there needs to be more mass deficiency if the 'slab' is not infinite in order to produce the same anomaly (see, for example, the Cheshire Basin model in Section 2.3.3).

(c) This is one of the strongest points made in Section 2.3.3, and it clearly applies to the western boundaries of the Moray Firth and Worcester Basins, the eastern boundary of the Cheshire Basin, and probably also the North Celtic Sea Basin.

(d) Reference to Figure 2.10 demonstrates that a small magnetic low north of a stronger positive anomaly is just what we expect if the source has induced magnetization or NRM parallel to the Earth's present field.

(e) Regionally, Moine and Dalradian metasediments are most important, but locally, such as around the Cairngorm–Aberdeen and Etive–Rannoch Moor granites, the low densities of these intrusions becomes more important.

(f) This is the situation described in detail in the Southern Caledonides part of Section 2.3.2—see also Figure 2.22c and Plate 1.2 for contrasts.

SAQ 2.3 (a) NW–SE gravity highs and magnetic rough zones beneath eastern England provide clues to the depth of shallow crystalline basement beneath younger cover. There are three main parallel ridges—the extension of the London–Brabant massif towards the Midlands (terminating around GR400300), the ridge that extends from East Anglia via exposed basement in Leicestershire to the Lake District, and a third ridge in the North Sea area (on the gravity map only) which appears to just graze North Yorkshire. These trends in eastern England turn towards NE–SW about a N–S line roughly along easting 360. NE–SW oriented basement ridges in the west occur in the Irish Sea, through Anglesey and North Wales and through central to South Wales.

(b) Geological data from isolated outcrops and boreholes suggest that the late Precambrian (Cadomian) ages extend north only so far as central England (somewhere between northings 300 and 400). Outside this area, potential field anomalies interpreted as basement ridges must be developed in Lower Palaeozoic strata. There is a suggestion that the Midlands Craton is roughly triangular, pointing north (cf. Figure 2.13), and that younger Caledonian basement is wrapped around it in an arcuate fashion (discussion in Section 2.3.1).

SAQ 2.4 (a) The magnetic field across the plateau lava fields of Skye, Mull and Antrim generates strong, narrow negative anomalies due to thin (shallow sources) that could only arise if they contain a reversed NRM.

(b) The negative gravity anomaly associated with this batholith clearly continues past Land's End, although the magnitude of the anomaly decreases as compared with outcropping granite areas in Devon and Cornwall.

(c) A ground-based magnetic survey (Figure 2.20c) with better resolution than aeromagnetic data reveals two anomalous zones on the flanks of the intrusion where thermal metamorphism has magnetized country rocks (the Borrowdale Volcanics).

(d) There is no significant gravity anomaly over the Strath Halladale outcrop, so this deduction follows (see Section 2.3.2).

SAQ 3.1 a, c, d and f are true; b and e are false.

(a) This is one of the key points to emerge from Sections 3.1.2 and 3.2.2. Both the LISPB and MOIST/WINCH lines cross the Moine Thrust and the Great Glen Fault, for example (Figure 3.8 and 3.26e/3.30)—the reflection profiles show these structures to much better effect.

(b) As explained in Section 3.2.1. (cf. Figure 3.23), true dip on a seismic travel time–distance diagram is only generated in the process of migration.

(c) The close spatial association between sediment-filled half-grabens and underlying major structures, leading to a mechanistic relationship, is explained in Section 3.2.2, under *The Upper Crust*—cf. also Figure 3.27.

(d) This conclusion arises from the interpretation of some short seismic refraction lines in the Midland Valley, which yield P-wave velocities exceeding 6 km s^{-1} at depths of only 4 km (cf. Section 3.1.3 and Figure 3.13).

(e) There are alternative mechanisms to brittle failure, whereby fault structures may continue as prominent reflectors across ductile zones; for example the existence of shear zones as depicted in Figure 3.42 (cf. Section 3.2.5).

(f) This is the final stage of the model developed in Section 3.2.3 and illustrated in Figure 3.38 and 3.39d. It seems likely that arc-related crust of the southern continent was thrust over the suture, which is clearly imaged on WINCH and NEC at and below mid-crustal levels.

SAQ 3.2 (a) Reduced time–distance graphs applied to refraction seismic data sets plot $t - x/v_0$ against distance (x) where v_0 is a typical velocity for a particular layer of interest in the strata being considered (e.g. Figure 3.5). The arrivals from this layer will then plot as a horizontal line in such a diagram and the degree of inclination of arrivals from all other layers gives an immediate visual impression of their seismic velocity relative to the v_0 layer. A reduced time-scale (say -10 s to $+10$ s out to

200–300 km) is another advantage of this approach, whereas an unreduced plot would be much more unwieldy (perhaps requiring a scale of 0–40 s).

(b) This technique applies to CMP surveying in which each source–detector pair produces arrivals at progressively greater times the further apart the source and detector are. Normal move-out corrections are applied to calculate the two-way time as though the source and detector were both at the CMP (i.e. at zero offset time, cf. Figure 3.21). The different arrivals are then stacked to reduce noise and improve the signal quality.

(c) Seismic modelling is the process whereby a velocity–depth structure is assumed; it is ray-traced to produce synthetic seismic sections, which are compared with that observed; the structure is then adjusted, retraced, etc. until a satisfactory fit is achieved—see Section 3.2.1.

SAQ 3.3 (a) The answer to this question depends on calculating the reflection coefficient for rocks on either side of the thrust. Acoustic impedence values (equation 3.5—density and velocity from Table 2.2) are as follows:

rhyolite 8.32×10^6 kg m^{-2} s^{-1}; shale 6.84×10^6 kg m^{-2} s^{-1}
(taking average wave speed)

gabbro 20.45×10^6 kg m^{-2} s^{-1}; peridotite 25.2×10^6 kg m^{-2} s^{-1}

Equation 3.6 then gives maximum and minimum reflection coefficient values across the thrust of:

R_{min} between rhyolite and gabbro $= \dfrac{20.45 - 8.32}{20.45 + 8.32} = 0.42$

R_{max} between shale and peridotite $= \dfrac{25.2 - 6.84}{25.2 + 6.84} = 0.57$.

Since a reflection coefficient greater than 0.2 gives a very strong reflection (Section 3.2.1), it follows that this thrust should be recorded with very prominent signals.

(b) Geologically, the thrust dips at 20°. In equation 3.7—sin $a = \tan \beta$—the angle β refers to the apparent (unmigrated) dip we want to know, while a refers to the true (migrated seismic section) dip.

Thus, we have $\tan \beta = \sin 20° = 0.342$

whence $\beta = 18.9°$

So the dip on an unmigrated section will be 18.9°.

(c) Dipping fault structures across which there is a strong reflection coefficient on seismic sections tend to produce *diffractions* (e.g. Figure 3.17) prior to migration.

SAQ 3.4 (a) From equation 3.5, the differing densities will produce an impedance contrast between the rocks, so at least part of the wave will be reflected at the interface and part will be transmitted. However, the transmitted part of the wave will not be refracted because there is no velocity contrast across the interface. (The latter conclusion follows Snell's law which we have not reiterated in this course: sin i/sin $r = v_1/v_2$ which in this case is unity, whence i, the angle of incidence $= r$, the angle of refraction.)

(b) In this case, there will again be some reflection, because there is an impedance contrast, but this time the transmitted wave will be refracted because of the velocity contrast across the interface. This assumes, of course, that the wave strikes the interface at an angle less than or equal to the critical angle (equation 3.1). (Award yourself a bonus if you realized that the elastic moduli of the rocks on either side of the interface would have to be different in order for their propagation velocities to differ with density remaining constant.)

SAQ 3.5 (a) These are reflections of the type labelled c in Figures 3.6 and 3.7; the raw data at the left of the LISPB seismogram compilation show a marked increase in amplitude at this point.

(b) The WINCH and MOIST profiles both contain dipping reflectors in the upper mantle down to *c*. 50 km depth, but the DRUM line, recorded to 30 s TWT, equivalent to *c*. 110 km depth, contains reflections due to the Flannan Thrust throughout much of its depth extent (cf. Section 3.2.2 and Figure 3.26f).

(c) This conclusion arises from the geological interpretation of the NEC seismic section (Figure 3.37) in which it appears that reflectors P1 and P2 mark the boundaries of a subduction complex that was tectonically smeared out beneath the northern continent, during ocean closure, and even penetrated the Moho beneath the Midland Valley.

(d) The Lizard–Start Thrust is correlated with reflector F on SWAT seismic lines 8 and 9 (Figure 3.41); it is probably overlain by high-density rocks—hence the gravity anomaly. However, a sedimentary basin has formed above high-density basement— hence the low-density rocks near the surface.

FURTHER READING

CHACKSFIELD, B. (1987) Gravity plumbs Britain's hidden geology. *New Scientist* **116**, 48–52.

A review of modern gravity data analysis and map production.

FREEMAN, B., KLEMPERER, S. L. AND HOBBS, R. W. (1988) The deep structure of the northern England and Iapetus suture zone from BIRPS deep seismic reflection profiles. *J. geol. Soc. Lond.* **145**, 727–740.

Detailed review of the topics covered in Section 3.2.3 and the source of the NEC seismic section.

KEAREY, P. AND BROOKS, M. (1984) *An Introduction to Geophysical Exploration.* Blackwell Scientific Publications, 296 pp.

Basic text covering theoretical aspects of all geophysical techniques in a modern context.

KLEMPERER, S. L. AND FIFIELD, R. (1988) Sound waves reflect Britain's deep geology. *New Scientist* **117** (No. 1598), 73–78.

A review of BIRPS techniques and discoveries at an accessible level.

LEE, M. K., PHARAOH, T. C. AND SOPER, N. J. (1990) Structural trends in central Britain from images of gravity and aeromagnetic fields. *J. geol. Soc. Lond.*, in press.

An advanced treatment of image analysis interpretation of potential field data in the UK–a very important paper.

OPEN UNIVERSITY, (1987) S338, Block 3, Part I Geophysical techniques OU Press, 131 pp.